Andreas Schild

Are the US ready for Peace with North Korea?

Engagement or Confrontation

tredition®

www.tredition.de

© 2018 Andreas Schild

Verlag und Druck: tredition GmbH, Hamburg

ISBN
Paperback: 978-3-7469-3127-2

Contents:

Introduction   p. 5

1. The Challenge of getting Reliable Information p. 9
   1.1.   Unknown North Korea
   1.2.   The weight of History   p. 17
   1.3.   After the End of Cold War   p. 27
   1.4.   The International Position of North Korea
                                             p. 36
   1.5.   The Urgency of Reforms   p. 39

2. From emergency Aid to Development Cooperation
                                             p. 43
   2.1.   Another Perspective
   2.2.   Trying to push the Door Open   p. 58
   2.3.   Preparing for a Round- Table Meeting   p. 78

3. A Vote for Engagement   p. 91

   3.1.   Common wisdom Questioned
   3.2.   North Korea's Stumbling Towards Recognition
                                             p.101
   3.3.   Policy Alternatives   p.108
   3.4.   Why President Trump might succeed   p.116

Bibliography   p. 118

Sources of the pictures: Front page, pages 72, 74 Erich Ober-holzer

p.28, 29, 81 Bernard Joos

p. 32, 35 Andreas Schild

Cover   The oxen driven ploughs experienced a renaissance as the Chollima tractors produced in the country since 1958 were not adapted to sloping land.

Introduction

The Korean Peninsula and particularly North Korea have been a hot-spot of regional and world politics since World War II. The Korean War was concluded in 1953 with an armistice which was not followed by a peace agreement.[1] The end of the Cold War brought the collapse of the communist system of governance and COMECON, the common market of the socialist block. North Korea remained a single remnant with the communist system in place and the same elite in power.

For almost 30 years, the debate on North Korea in the West has been dominated by the dilemma between engagement and confrontation. Under the leadership of the United States the prevailing position, with some rare exceptions, has been rather confrontation or certainly the absence of a political will for engagement.

Dealing with North Korea unavoidably hits the stumbling block of missing basic data and reliable information about the country. This difficulty has been cultivated and fostered by the North Korean authorities. The country today has the reputation of being a "hermit kingdom". The combination of isolation and being a hot-spot with tensions, military build-up and even danger of war have continuously generated rumours and brought the Korean peninsula to the front pages of the media.

The present paper is intended to contribute to a clearer view of North Korea.

---

[1] The armistice was signed by North Korea, China and the commander of the American troops but not by South Korea.

My point of departure is neither science nor politics but subjective experience and observation, which I tried to verify in retrospect by confronting my conclusions with literature and publications. This perspective has evolved through my stay in the country as the person responsible for a United Nations program and as consultant to a bilateral development agency. Working in a foreign culture and non-transparent political environment calls for a minimum of empathy or, worded in a perhaps more modern way, a "rational compassion"[2] in order to be efficient and effective. I want also to stress here a certain sensitivity of a citizen from a small country. I have learnt to be respectful and to try to understand other nations. This is not a moral position, even less a policy perception. From the point of view of a small country this is part of a survival strategy, which gives another perspective and another way of looking at things. Citizens of a world power can definitely afford to disregard such an attitude.

This background provokes me to question some traditional perceptions of the country and common wisdom shared by political scientists and journalists.

Writing about North Korea is a risky venture. Little is known about the country. On the other hand, a lot is being written. The mass media usually take over the opinion of the American mainstream. The state of knowledge is biased and communicated with stereotypes. Even the usual sympathy for a small country normally shown by the Swiss does not work in the case of North Korea.[3]

Anticipating that my position will largely be judged as subjective, incomplete and biased, I want to emphasize that North Korea is not my country. The political culture and system cannot be further away from what

---

[2] Paul Bloom, Against Empathy, The Case for Rational Compassion, London 2016

[3] The Swiss delegation for the Olympic Games in South Korea included a former commander of the Swiss Delegation of the Neutral Nations Supervisory Commission for the control of the armistice. In a TV interview the journalist asked the athletes whether they felt secure so close to North Korea.

I am aspiring to and what I like. I strongly believe in personal freedom and autonomy of local and smaller units and in a decentralized governance structure. I think also that any political system needs mechanisms of checks and balances: this I badly miss in North Korea. Any political system based on heritage of power develops a bigotry, which is hardly compatible with a democratic vision.

However, I have developed a certain understanding for a system which has evolved in given circumstances and which has survived and been adapted against all odds. I do have a certain admiration for persons who work in this system and make an effort to improve it. Above all, as an intellectual, I have to show respect for this country. It is not only shaped by its leadership and "stone age "communism but also by geopolitical forces and is part of a global and regional power game.

In the first part I try to describe the state of knowledge and give a short historical overview of North Korea since its creation.

The second chapter relates my experience of working in the country. The focus is food security and how the Korean authorities and the international community have been dealing with it. I describe how change is happening without decisions being made.

The final chapter questions some basic assumptions and generally accepted perceptions of North Korea. It makes a cause for honest negotiations and engagement with the country. My conclusion is that the attitude of the western world under the leadership of the United States has had largely negative consequences instead of creating a conducive atmosphere on the Korean Peninsula and the potential for a peaceful solution.

A prerequisite for a sustainable and peaceful development on the Korean Peninsula is not only North Korea's compliance with international agreements and norms but also a change in American policy.

1. The Challenge of Getting Reliable Information

1.1.   Unknown North Korea

The State of Knowledge

I asked myself about the pertinence and use of editing impressions experienced 15 years ago. The amazing fact is that the picture we have of North Korea is almost the same as thirty years earlier. North Korea is an unknown country, its policies are enigmatic and the political system is a remnant of the past with no future. North Korea is alternatively named a rogue state or a "hermit kingdom" and a danger to world peace. The country is mostly presented as following irrational and irresponsible policies.

At first sight the geopolitical situation in North East Asia has not changed much either. The country remains isolated and the situation on the Korean Peninsula remains unstable.

For the external observer, it is astonishing that the knowledge of what is happening in the country has not substantially increased. Some interesting books have been written by   journalists and by researchers having access to Russian archives, closed up to now. The sources of information remain think-tanks which are either government- financed or are otherwise linked to governments and contain a substantial amount of political propaganda.   Interviews with defectors provide another source. These testimonies are interesting but it is not always possible to distinguish between the personal fate and the political context. One of the only books from a living experience in the country has been written by Felix Abt (A Capitalist in North Korea. My seven years in the hermit Kingdom). It did not receive the response it deserved.

There are however quite a substantial number of publications on North Korea. The main topics refer to the nuclear and missile capacity, the three- generation hereditary succession, human rights and the defector issue.

American and Japanese analyses are often influenced by a hostile stance towards North Korea. The research seems to be often disturbed by traditional stereotypes such as irrational behaviour and a stone-age system. These are also the topos flowing into newspaper reports of the Western press. According to a survey conducted by the Japanese government in 2015, over 86 % of the Japanese population consider the abdication issue the major area of interest regarding North Korea.

Information about North Korea accessible to the average citizen in the West has the tendency to be sensational and negatively biased: for example, the South Korean Secret Service reported in April 2014 that Hyong Yong-chol, the Minister of Defence, had been purged and shot with a four-barrel antiaircraft gun. This report is immediately a number-one news item in the international press. After only a few hours, the same service has doubts. A month later a South Korean spokesman says that the execution of the defence minister should be considered a rumour. Even American sources have serious doubts about the execution (see US-Korea Institute of John Hopkins University July 2014). [4]

---

[4] Another hype was the sinking of Choenan, a South Korean Corvette with more than forty casualties in March 2010. This accident was immediately attributed to an attack by a North Korean torpedo. However, in the first report of the defence ministry, no other boat was reported in the surrounding area. The joint Korean- American marine exercises also did not observe a boat. Within South Korea the issue remained highly controversial and the issue quickly became politicised. An international expert group of Western countries confirmed North Korean responsibility. A Russian and a Chinese investigation came to contrary conclusions. A Canadian University confirmed that the torpedo was of North Korean origins. However it has been lying in the water for at least six months

Even serious research with a minimum of compassion is based on secondary information or on official publications. Knowledge of the factual reality is rather rare and objectively speaking also difficult to investigate. [5] The North Korean authorities do actually very little to avoid the prevailing picture of North Korea as a secretive country.

An important source of information on North Korea has been Vantage Point, a publication by the South Korean press agency Yonhap, which was discontinued in 2016. Most of the articles were based on external observation and without access to primary data. But a lot of articles go beyond the unfriendly stereotypes and make an effort to understand and be objective.

If relations seem to be largely unchanged, the framework conditions and the situation in North Korea have changed substantially.

The Korean Peninsula - a Geopolitical Hotspot

From the beginning of the 21st century, political and international debate in Northeast Asia has been dominated by one topic: would the Democratic Popular Republic of Korea (DPRK) abandon its international isolation and become a part of the international community? The military build-up and particularly the capacity to develop nuclear weapons (WMD) has been a hot issue since the early 90s and led the countries involved to a tentative settlement by the Framework Agreement 1994.

---

[5] A typical formulation which can be found in various papers and repeatedly reads as follows – in Vantage Point February 2015, Development cooperation with North Korea by Moon Kyung -Yu: "North Korea watchers were making mixed evaluations of the North Korean Economy. In other words, some of them saw that the North Korean command economy based on production and distribution under a central plan was functioning in a normal way, while others believed that the socialist planned economy had already been partly eroded by the market economy."

Two weeks after the signing of the agreement, the American Congress was taken over by the Republicans. The Agreed Framework was declared a political orphan. The following years were characterized by the disastrous food security situation and diplomatic tensions.[6]

The beginning of the century started on a promising note. The immediate reason for this sudden optimism was labelled as "sunshine policy". 20 European countries established diplomatic relations. An important step was made by the visit of the President of South Korea to Pyongyang. This was followed by a number of symbolic gestures (e.g. the Prime Minister of Japan presented the regrets of his country for the atrocities committed by his country, particularly during World War II) which helped to thaw diplomatic relations in this part of the world. On the more discreet operational level, the contract for the construction of two light water reactors, a central piece of the Agreed Framework, was finally signed with ABB, a Switzerland- based company.

These diplomatic overtures were followed by initiatives on a more technical level. Some Western countries and particularly the United Nations, through its development programme (UNDP), explored the potential of enhanced international cooperation with North Korea.

The country had gone through a serious crisis first by the decay of the Soviet Union and particularly the end of COMECON, which constituted the market for virtually all North Korean products, and secondly by a period of drought and floods which produced a national disaster of hunger and a huge number of casualties. The international community responded with a largescale humanitarian assistance programme and particularly food aid. The World Food Programme (WFP) of the United Nations was the major player on the scene and its representative headed as Humanitarian Coordinator the UN operations in the country.

On the part of the UN family the assumption was that the sunshine policy would enable the UN organisations and the bilateral donors to

---

[6] Stephen Bosworth, former US Ambassador to South Korea, the first director of KEDO. See: www.money.CNN 5.12.2003

change gear from a humanitarian assistance mode to long term development cooperation.

Anticipating the results of these initiatives, we have to accept that they failed dramatically. Geopolitics and changes within the main partner countries through elections and policy changes created again a frosty international environment and North Korea was not ready to play according to the rules of the game defined by the international community under the leadership of the United States. North Korea was added to the "axis of evil" countries by President Bush and, as happened in Iraq, feared the risk of being invaded.

Since 2017 North Korea has again put itself in the forefront of international media with nuclear tests and ballistic experiments. The increased military capacity of North Korea, with the threat of being able to use missiles which can reach US territory, has increased the concern of the United States. With the mutual threatening with the famous Red Button (and its size) by the leaders of both states, we are aware that the situation has seriously aggravated.

Two aspects deserve special attention beyond the situation on the Korean Peninsula:
- The fact that the present US administration explicitly states that they will no longer impose their views on democracy in other countries is certainly good news for North Korea: it will be easier to find an agreement if governance and human rights are excluded from the agenda.

- The economic development in North East Asia presently shows us another feature: clearly the western capitalism based on democracy and transparency is not the only path to the future. Scholars of the region are not seeing western type democracy as an objective: they see that the former socialist countries do not absolutely need a change of regime. They see an option in reform conducted by the present regime without any change in the political system. East Asia today demonstrates that economic development and improvement of the living conditions of the population does not require a western type of democracy. They tend to see in North Korea a "low level regime reform" i.e. reform lead by the regime and elite in place.

Positive Developments Underreported.

Authors with confirmed knowledge in situ, such as Rüdiger Frank, Felix Abt or Kathy Zellweger, in their thorough analysis of the present situation, observe that the Koreans seem to be better off than a couple of years ago. All of a sudden nobody speaks of hunger even though the WFP programme has been suspended and we remained perplexed about the six million hungry people WFP have been continuously reporting. The scaling down of a UN presence has been digested fairly well. The severity of the UN- decided sanction measures has almost been proportionate to the increase of the wellbeing of the population. It can be safely assumed that the sanctions imposed by the Security Council have been outweighed by the effects of globalization. Even China has very successful business people, whose activities abroad cannot or are not controlled by government. The lack of global governance rules apparently makes sanctions look redundant. Ironically, globalization seems to help the isolated country.

External factors have had a decisive influence on North Korea. It seems they worked rather in favour of the country during the last couple of years: China has become the second largest economy of the globe. It wants to avoid two things: American presence on the mainland border and the nuclear bomb on the Korean Peninsula.

Russia has recovered from the post-soviet crisis. During the last few years, relations with North Korea have steadily improved. But the level of commercial exchange with China is much higher. No settlement on the Korean peninsula is possible without the two countries. They have one feature in common: they will not formulate any conditionality concerning governance, human rights or democracy. This again helps North Korea. The elite do not have to fear any pressure for internal reforms from their their neighbours. In addition, both are rather examples of how economic growth is possible with a predominant role of the state and one party. This is actually the message that the North Koreans like to hear.

The US and their allies have in the meantime lost the leverage to dictate the negotiation agenda. This chance was missed 15 years ago. Today, America wants to do business. Their interest has been reduced to one simple issue: the military power of North Korea and the threat of its missiles. They want China to help take North Korea's missiles away, but helping the US is not in in China's text book.

The position of North Korea has been strengthened during the last 15 years. The economic situation of the normal citizen has improved and the military capability in terms of missiles and nuclear devices has increased. The tone of its declarations has become more assertive.

North Korea a Stunting Orphan?

My entry point in North Korea was the Sunshine Policy and the post-emergency situation after the natural disasters of 1995/6 and the famine. Food security continues to be a challenge today. This is not only due to failing policies and lacking incentives but also due to the concrete environmental and agro-ecological situation and, evidently, the international sanctions imposed on the country.

Energy supply is insufficient, industrial production lacks spare parts and needs a serious technological boost. Infrastructure requires very high and long-term investments the country does not have and has no chance of acquiring.

The human rights situation is a permanent issue. All external sources agree in their poor rating. Only countries like Syria, Yemen and Libya are rated worse. North Korea has not been able to react in a positive and cooperative way to international pressure. The government is asking from its citizens discipline, subordination and renunciation of goods and services which we in the West and even the North East Asian neighbours would take for granted.

For the North Korean authorities, the continued questioning of the human rights situation is a permanent nuisance. They consider themselves not being treated in a fair way. They feel that the way the Japanese treated the Koreans till 1945 was not better and they are treating the political opponents not very differently from South Korea under Syngman Rhee or General Park Chung-Hee. In their opinion, the international community is not using a similar yardstick for China.[7] They are judged by the international community in a biased way.

---

[7] The UN had conducted a study on human rights violation in North Korea. The story of Shin Dong-hyuk, a highly profiled defector, served as a basis for the report published in December 2014. But in January 2015 Shin had to excuse himself. He acknowledged that parts of his story were incorrect

Is it surprising that North Korea feels that the human rights issue is just used for political reasons as an excuse?

1.2.   The Weight of History

The Geographic Setting

The largest part of the Korean Peninsula lies between the 35th and 40th latitude. The capital of North Korea, Pyongyang, is situated on the same latitude as Sicily or Washington. The climate is characterized by two extremes: during winter by the severe cold of Siberia, during summer by subtropical temperatures. The consequence of this special situation is that multiannual plants like trees are comparable with the temperate climate of Europe whereas the annual plants have a subtropical character.

The very pronounced changes of temperature influence agricultural production and productivity at different altitudes. The vegetation pattern is strongly imprinted by the north- south, and east–west exposure and altitude. The precipitation pattern may change from year to year. Korea lies outside the influence of monsoon rains but within the reach of the summer typhoons. They influence the precipitation regime with substantial irregularities.

Rainfall can locally be very strong with floods but neighbouring areas may suffer from drought. Generally speaking, precipitation patterns in summer are unstable.

Culturally speaking, Korea belongs to the influence area of Confucianism. Even today, social behaviour and organisation are consistent with neo-Confucian values, which experienced a revival in the 19th century. This was strengthened during the Japanese occupation after 1910. It became a central expression of Korean identity and received the status of cultural self-determination against the occupying power.

The social structure of Korea was historically always imprinted by the outspoken and strong difference between landlords and simple farmers. These have traditionally been subject to a massive exploitation and have few rights. In the period of World War II, 18% of the farmers had land of their own. The remaining 82% worked the land as tenants or agricultural labourers. During the Japanese occupation, the production of rice was strongly forced. At independence, rice formed 30 % of the agricultural production.

As a matter of fact, Korea was such a backyard during the war that the two decisive powers had no strategy and no plans for it. When the Russians landed in Wonsan after the surprising capitulation of Japan, they hadn't even Korean speaking interpreters and had to mobilize Korean immigrants in Central Asia. The US had no plans to get involved on the Asian mainland. Their strategy at the time was to control strategic islands.

After partition, virtually all the industry of the country was in the northern part. It had an immense overweight in hard and brown coal, iron ore and magnesite as well as a large potential for hydro- energy and a well-developed infrastructure.

The South got the majority of good agricultural land. The North was attributed 124'818 square kilometres, roughly 56,5% of the total surface and about half of the agricultural land. However, only 25% of irrigated rice land belonged to the North. The yields per hectare in the southern provinces were 25% above the yields in the north (for irrigation as well as for rain-fed agriculture).

At the moment of partition approximately 9 Million people lived in the North. Returning Koreans from Manchuria and Japan substantially increased the population of the South. The population in the North, thanks to the well-organised industrial workers, remained well-structured and fairly stable. The South had no such tradition. However, technocrats, engineers and technicians left the North. Approximately 9'000 to 10'000 Japanese specialists left the country. It is estimated that a total of 15'000 trained technicians migrated from the North.

The Political System

North Korea is governed by a top-down, centralized, authoritarian system. Since its   foundation the country has been strongly militarized. The role and liberty of the individual citizen are strongly restricted and the individual has to submit to the interest of the common cause, which is defined by a small elite. Society is controlled by a strong secret service but also by a network of self-controlled communities.

To conclude that the system is perceived by the population as a communist
suppression, as western journalists and observers tend to think is an illusion. Koreans have never experienced a western age of enlightenment and large parts of the population have always lived without individual rights. To understand Korean society, it must be borne in mind that the cultural past should not be interpreted with a western perception of human rights and democracy.

Four aspects may help to understand the situation:
-    The regime in the North under Kim Il Sung enjoyed after 1945 a larger base of legitimization than the military rulers of the South. The anti-colonial past of Kim Il Sung created an aura which was cleverly built into the national determination of the young country. It shaped also an ideological basis for the Korean War, which could be justified as a battle against the foreign element in the South which hindered the unification of the nation. We can also surmise that the access to agricultural land in the South was a strong motif for the northern government. The North, with its strong industrial basis, was hardly seen self-reliant in terms of food production. So much so that external experts declared the North Korean state as not viable. It seems that the North Korean aggression was welcomed by a substantial part of the population in the South as well as by the Koreans in Japan.

- The missing peace agreement means that North Korea considers itself technically still at war.[8] This justifies the high degree of mobilization and the fact that the army is virtually the most important organ of the state. The permanent fear of an aggression created a psychological situation where the army had an overriding role for guaranteeing protection against foreign aggression. With the failure of the opening up of the country and the aborted Framework Agreement, Kim Jong-Il, the son of the great leader, with the Shogun (army first) policy, created with the army the guarantee for national independence.[9]

- Western observers consider the Workers Party, the communist party, and with it the „Stalinist regime", as the main stumbling block for a peaceful development on the Peninsula. The press still uses the term "stone age communism ". The rigid hierarchical structure of the state with its cellular tight structure can be looked at as a model for a traditional communist organisation. The party is certainly after the Army the second most important organisation in the country. The structure of the party helps to extend a network of control and communication for the whole country. On the other hand, there has been no national party assembly for a decade. After the end of the Cold War the party made some declarations regarding opening up the country, but since the early 90s the

---

[8] 1953 the armistice agreement was considered a first step. It should have been followed by a peace agreement. The Geneva conference in 1954 brought no solution.

[9] As North Korea was classified as a rogue state and part of the axis of evil and the invasion of Iraq left no doubt to the Korean public of the essence of this policy.

party hardly was in a position to suggest creative answers for its problems.[10]

- From the outside, we perceive the personality cult as the third fundament of the power structure in North Korea. Within the country, it leads to rituals which are hardly understandable for the western Cartesian mind. The worship of the founder of the nation and his successor looks very artificial. Those who have had the chance to travel by car in remote areas with little outside contact, get an impression of how deeply authority is looked up to: the persons on the border of the road welcome your car with a deep Kowtow hardly compatible with egalitarian communist behaviour.

  The leadership and the state ceremonies borrow heavily from the Confucian past: the symbols surrounding authority and the deference. What the state asks from the citizen is not very different from what the population knows from the past and is deeply rooted in traditions which also reveal the imperial cosmogony of its history. This attitude and value system is also part of the national awakening since the occupation by the colonial power and the leadership plays with it with virtuosity.

  To ignore these interdependencies might lead to wrong interpretations of the present political ruling system and its fundamentals anchored in the Korean soul.

It is dangerous to formulate hypotheses at this point. Interpreting the period after the Cold War, it seems that new initiatives and ideas have

---

[10] This situation changed only with the taking over of the third Kim, Kim Sung Un. His emphasis on economic development and the purging of the army leadership seems to indicate a shift in the power structure. At the same time, it is noteworthy that the party has lost some of the traditional reference to the founding fathers of communism and their basic principles

come out from an inner circle around the supreme leadership. It does not mean that the leader has an unrestricted power for change. There are early birds, who, thanks to their personal status, make small trials and take liberties, which can eventually be converted into official policy. However, such steps can be preceded by a lot of discussion in the different powerhouses- the army, the party, the state security and the ministries.

It seems that in this game the family of the leadership and the surrounding clientele are more and more significant for the future development of the country. The evolutionary process will not lead to a democratic, pluralistic system. It will remain fairly autocratic with the ruling elite very careful not to lose any influence. The gurus for such an evolution are not in the West or the South. China and Vietnam are the proven examples of how reform is possible without the elite changing the political system.

Support from the Socialist World

Here it is not intended to describe the history of North Korea since 1945. It might however be worthwhile to identify certain trends and patterns prevailing before 1991 and to see whether they help to explain the situation after the end of the Cold War and to understand the efforts to overcome the crisis of the 90s.

After 1945 North Korea received massive economic and technical support from the socialist countries. Exact figures from 1945 to 49 are available from China and Russia. During the Korean War the support was part of the war effort. It included not only food, weapons and ammunition but also combatant troops (from China) and air force support (from Russia).

For the reconstruction phase after the war the socialist brother countries had to make hard sacrifices - they were themselves in a phase of reconstruction - the volume of which was probably not fully known by their own population.[11] [12]

---

[11] The armistice negotiations reached their concluding stage in May- June 1953. The revolt of the Berlin workers started 17 June. The armistice was signed by the US army (on behalf of UN), North Korea and China, but not by South Korea. Actually, Syngman Rhee opposed the armistice.

[12] Ingeborg Göthel, Geschichte Koreas. Berlin 1978, p. 312 ff, describes the support provided by the socialist states including the German Democratic Republic, which was considered as the socialist spearhead in the west.

At the beginning, whole cities with the corresponding infrastructure were built on a turnkey basis. (The socialist Germany rebuilt the industrial city Hamhung, a steel complex (Hwanghä) and an industrial complex in Pyongyang). This was followed by a period of building industrial

enterprises with the same approach. The Korean staff was trained and partly invited for education to the donor country.

Up to the 80s the following pattern seemed to prevail:
- Building-up of a production unit based on a punctual demand. There was hardly any integration into the general economy. Little attention was given to the ancillary industry.
- There was no provision for renewal or repair. After a certain period, the unit was replaced by a new one.
- Apparently, political leadership and the technicians in the enterprises were not   connected. The planning of targets was the responsibility of the political leadership and not of the management of the enterprise. Apparently, there was no management layer responsibility between technicians and political leaders.

Till 1991 the embassies of the socialist countries included a large staff of technical and scientific specialists, who functioned practically as development experts. [13]

---

[13] The compound of the embassy of the Democratic Republic of Germany included tennis courts, swimming pool, cinema hall and staff quarters. After 2001 all the EU embassies with staff quarters were housed in this „gated community" and could not fill it.

The North Korean Perception of the Socialist Countries

The basic self-understanding of Korean culture entails a clearly reserved attitude towards and even rejection of everything foreign. This mentality became more confirmed during the Japanese occupation (and might be an explanation for the ambiguous attitude of the South Koreans towards the Americans).

This background explains the following elements which might help to create a mosaic to understand the situation:

- The basic norm aiming at an autonomous self-relying style can be observed in all ways of life and goes beyond political considerations and the perception of the external word. Production, particularly in agriculture, is organised so as to permit a high degree of local autarchy (self-sufficiency). At the beginning of the 21st century, no regular flight connexions had been established between mayor cities.
- Eyewitnesses from the socialist brother states report for the period before 1991 the lack of coherent information and the missing access to basic data. Apparently, the socialist development cooperation had to deal with problems similar to the capitalist variety.
- An important cornerstone in the evolution of North Korean political philosophy was the Sino – Russian conflict. In the immediate term, North Korea undertook efforts to avoid being drawn into the conflict. The conflict between the two leading communist powers supporting and protecting North Korea created an ideological crisis. The regime organised a thorough purge. The main target groups were the academicians sent for training in socialist countries. All of them were called back and most of them were sent into subordinate positions in faraway places.

Some authors quote the supreme leader already in the late 40s as explaining the need for self- reliance. The Sino-soviet conflict has accelerated the process of elaborating "Juche" as the national philosophy and the golden path to choose for the future of North Korea.[14]

---

[14] Scholars call "Juche" the national philosophy of North Korea. The author is Kim Il Sung. Juche has roughly speaking three dimensions: A political (sovereignty), economic (self-sufficiency or self-reliance) and military (autonomy). Some authors date Juche back to the end of the Korean War and call it a new religion. As far as I know, Juche appeared as a term already end of the 40s. My reading is that Juche became the national ideology as a reaction of the Sino – Soviet conflict, when North Korea needed a political value system of its own.

Maybe it is premature to make a clear statement at this stage. The speeches (and the appearance including the dress code) show under Kim Jong un a clear renaissance of the importance of Juche. The frequent references to Juche go along with the disappearance of the hard core communist terminology in the speeches of the new leader.

1.3. After the End of the Cold War

The lack of reliable data and of analytical reports which are not politically biased make it   difficult to analyse the crisis generated by the end of the Cold War in North Korea.

The official line of argument pertains to two different changes:

- North Korea is a highly industrialized country. Due to the economic blockade and the politics of the United States, the country is temporarily undergoing a crisis. This is a transitory period which has been imposed on the country and does not require any internal reforms.
- The floods and droughts 1995/6 were the result of a natural disaster due to climate change. The international community is welcome to participate in a transitory and punctual mission to help North Korea to overcome this human and natural crisis.

All indications lead however to the conclusion that the end of the Cold War and the natural disasters were rather the culmination of a structural crisis, which became visible from the mid 80s.

With the growing crisis in the socialist block, the capacity to renew enterprises in the modern sector in North Korea decreased rapidly. The whole productive sector already suffered in 1991 from a lack of repair and technological deficit. As the end of COMECON, the latter was not replaced by the world market, the isolation was also felt in the form of a lack of capacity to invest. Some industries like the coal mines, but a lso electricity production, still used the capacity and technology installed by the Japanese.

With the floods of 1995 the industrial production fell completely in disarray. According to authorities, the coal mines have been flooded in such a way that pits can no longer be rescued. Some experts considered the technology hopelessly beyond repair, and that only new investment could save the industry.

These are construction sites of the same hydro project with three different levels of power generation. On the left the management has probably called for a demonstration of popular enthusiasm for the visiting authorities from the Capital. The local people apparently do not take it very seriously but they do not look unhappy. The picture on the right shows the construction higher up of an earthen dam. According to international experts the plans are state of the art. Both pictures show a complete absence of technical equipment and earthmoving machines.

The end of the Soviet Union and the decomposition of the socialist block with the COMECON meant a loss of the traditional market for North Korean industry and trade. This loss radically changed the economic and political framework conditions. It was not just the market which disappeared.

This structural crisis of industry splashed over to the fragile agriculture, which functioned traditionally thanks to cheap energy prices and subsidies from the industrial sector.

Food Security questioned

Self-sufficiency of food production was considered a basic challenge for the country from 1945. The official planning figures for agricultural production show the tendency to increase the surface of productive land. Regions such as Deodang and Miru Hills have been cleared and converted into agricultural land. High priority was given to the expansion of rice production. Till 1949 the surface had been increased by 25% and in 1949 the country is for the first time declared self-sufficient. The good performance seems to be due to the first land reform in 1948: large land holdings were split and redistributed with a maximum size of 5 hectares.

From 1960 to 64, a big land reform was introduced. The agricultural production was collectivized and organized in large cooperatives. The purpose was an accelerated modernization with the slogans "irrigation, mechanization, chemicalization and electrification". Terrains were moved and converted into irrigated land. More than 100'000 hectares were reclaimed from the sea in the coastal areas.

1978 was officially celebrated as the first year when self-sufficiency was reached. The grain harvest was given as 8 million tons. The planning figures gave a target of 10 million tons for 1984.

In spite of all the efforts of agricultural modernization, food security remained a precarious sector of the national economy.

The crisis of North Korea can be demonstrated easily using agriculture as an example. Agriculture and food security became the main reason for an unexpected presence of western organisations in the country. Hunger and death brought North Korea also on to the radar of the general public.

Probably the incipient crisis and the nuclear crisis are interrelated. The second was used to mitigate the first. Already in 1992, during the negotiations to end the nuclear issue, the Korean Government asked for the provision of food as a compensation for neutralizing its nuclear plant. The final version of the framework agreement made a provision for heavy oil supply. Since then food and fertilizer have been supplied.

In 1993, the authorities changed the priorities for the 7 years plan and put agricultural production for the first time as top priority for the coming three years. These are clear indicators that the government had problems with running agriculture in such a way that food security could be assured.

From the available information, it is not possible to establish clearly whether self- sufficiency was really reached. According to IRRI statistics, North Korea had a surplus of rice in 1987. Since then the country was a regular importer of rice from Thailand. At the beginning of the 90s it seems that the supply chain for agriculture fell apart. Lorries could no longer be finished in the factory due to missing parts and energy, the tractor factory stopped producing in 1994. The two fertilizer factories were no longer functional.

The modern agriculture introduced in the 60s now showed clear structural problems: modernization was built on modern technology with cheap energy. It followed largely the model of the Green Revolution. The industrial crisis was also an energy crisis. Cheap energy as a backbone for irrigation was no longer available. As an example, the situation of Miru Hills can be described: the water had to be lifted in 12 stages in order to produce only a mediocre rice harvest. The lack of energy, water and agrochemicals made a rice production based on irrigation a virtually impossible option. [15]

Farmers use a maximum of flexibility. The picture shows how beans are planted outside the borders of the family garden which is allowed by the system. The stickles lean towards the inside and are considered part of the family garden. See also the slopes behind the farm. They are cultivated and the harvest is not part of the official planning figures and help the farmer to supplement his diet and family budget. (Mai 2002)

---

[15] The study conducted for the preparation of a Round Table Conference showed that North Korea in 2000 produced only 27% of the energy produced in 1989.

exclusively on the calorie dimension of food security. Oils, proteins vitamins and minerals are not considered.   The structural problem is not quantity but quality of food. Even during the most comfortable period of the DPRK meat had to be imported

Farmers still have potatoes in stock of last year's harvest which they convert into starch (Mai 2002)

1.4. The International Position of North Korea

The Relations with Neighbours

Since its foundation, North Korea entertains officially cordial and friendly relations with the two socialist countries China and Russia. In discussing with Koreans, I always felt a certain uneasiness with regard to China. The Chinese had virtually rescued the country in the Korean War and paid their support with an enormous loss of human life. Officially this vital contribution was recognised by the North Koreans only late and quite hesitantly. The common perception is that China is the secret ally of North Korea. Certainly, the country could not have survived the hard regime of the sanctions imposed by the Security Council without China. But the North Koreans do not trust the Chinese. It seems to be the attitude of the small country towards a big neighbour. History plays its role: the Korean king had to pay tributes to the Chinese emperor. The relation was not very much different from that of Tibet. The Koreans are very aware of this legacy. With Russia, the relation is less of a problem. Since the end of Cold War, however, relations have sunk to a very low level. This is gradually changing since the recovery of Russia under President Putin.

The relations with South Korea can hardly be summed up in a few sentences. Since World War II the North pretends to be the real and legitimate representative of the Korean   nation. This was a view largely shared by most Koreans: Kim Il Sung could base his power on the anti-colonial fight in Manchuria, whereas in the South the American Army had nobody to put in power. They had to fly in a president who was residing in the US. He and a large number of the officials and the police had a reputation of being followers of the hated colonial power. At the end of the Korean War the American Commander signed the armistice agreement. Synman Rhee, the President of the South, refused to sign. Today North Korea considers itself still technically at war. North Korea even today considers the South as the extended arm of the US and thinks that peace conditions have to be negotiated with the US.

Japan is the former colonial power which exploited Korea economically and suppressed Korean culture. Between 80'000 and 120'000 Korean girls and women were kidnapped and misused as prostitutes by the Japanese army. North Korea asks for an apology and compensation for the injustice done. The Japanese government has done so in the South. With the North, the Japanese authorities, as a precondition, asked for an explanation as to what happed to the Japanese abductees who were kidnapped by the North Korean secret service.

The non-existence of a peace agreement has not only far reaching consequences for external relations but also for interior politics. The issue of state security has given the justification for a strong position of the army in the decision-making process. The American military interventions in Afghanistan, Kuwait and Iraq constitute a very understandable justification base; this view is largely shared by the majority of North Koreans.

Of special interest are some economic considerations. The neighbours have all the interest to integrate North Korea into the North Eastern Economic space and see in such an integration a solution of some pending issues. Among the projects is the opening of a railway crossing the 38th parallel. South Korea expects a closer and more direct access to the oil reserves of Siberia and some studies show a good potential for a direct railway connexion between Pusan and Amsterdam.

The Relations with Western Countries

The position of the United States is the corner stone for the situation of North Korea. After 1945 they eliminated in the South directly and indirectly the workers groups and individuals who were supporting the North. The United States were the ones stopping the reunification aimed at by the North in the Korean War and in the view of North Korea they are the main stumbling block hindering access to the international market. Thanks to their influence in the International Financial Institutions (World Bank, Asian Development Bank) they block the access to international credit. The rehabilitation of the infrastructure is not possible without international investments. A precondition for the North is the establishment of diplomatic relations with the US. Even being treated as a rogue state by Reagan and as part of the Axis of Evil by Bush, the North is interested in having regular relations with the US. The condition sine qua non is to be recognised as equal partner and not to accept preconditions.

The position of the European countries is of special interest. With the Sunshine Policy, 20 European nations established diplomatic relations with North Korea and opened embassies in Pyongyang in 2000. North Korea sees its relations with EU and the European countries as non-problematic and positive. For the European countries, however, a successful process on reconciliation with the South is a precondition for more intensive relations.

1.5.   The Urgency of Internal Reforms

The requirement for reforms is perceived very differently according to points of view. The European observer puts governance and human rights in the centre. Americans and the immediate neighbours put the renouncement of weapons of mass destruction in the foreground. For North Koreans, the question is what is opportune without losing their identity and questioning the established power structure. They are convinced that the more they can demonstrate their military strength the more they are immune against foreign influence.

The need for reforms is therefore getting high priorities in the western view. This is opposite to the official Korean position. Its recipe is: no reforms, but making the system more efficient. I doubt that reform and the improvement of the human rights situation is a must due to internal pressure. Here the western experts might be wrong. This does not mean that the elite does not stand under enormous pressure. The source is less popular discontent than the aspirations of the new generation of the elite. Security and external policy issues make reforms very slow, or at least give the elite an excuse for delay.[17]

---

[17] This was my position beginning of 2002. I must say, when I left the country in September 2004 my impression was much more that reform was pushed from above. The Army and the State security were rather delaying everything. However, the biggest hurdle is mid-level staff. They have been either so much indoctrinated or think the present system is so convenient that they strongly oppose change. Putting into practice certain reforms needs staff at the implementation level who have to be trained in new orientations. I think we completely underestimated this aspect.

North Korea is no transition country, and even less a developing one.

The DPRK authorities want to play according to their own, or at least commonly agreed rules, and they think they can afford it. Nevertheless, the question is whether they really have their own vision and how far they are learning from other examples.

The unification of Germany or the reorganisation of the GIS states is definitely not a development the North Koreans are aiming at.

They are more impressed by the Chinese model and there are clear examples where we can see that North Korea is following the Chinese example. However North Korea has much less room for manoeuvring. It is not just a question of size but also of structure: according to statistics, 25 -31% of the population makes a living from agriculture. In China, we are speaking of 80%.

In China, an enormous industrial growth was possible due to cheap labour coming from the agricultural sector. In North Korea, there are no cheap labour reserves in agriculture. The country undergoes a big structural change. Agriculture might become more labour intensive. Finally, the economic reform in China started with some important changes in the top hierarchy. In North Korea, it is the long-established leadership who wants to change with the top hierarchy remaining in charge.

Reform cannot be called Reform

Our starting point was that the country needs reforms but the authorities remain in a dogmatic blind alley and do not move. I gradually became aware of the fact that if I do not see change, this does not mean that it does not happen. Since the end of the Cold War and particularly after the natural disasters a series of measures were taken by the authorities which were not known. This can be explained by some typical circumstances in North Korea. Firstly, the "experts" working so far in North Korea were experienced in short term immediate impact activities. Doing background research was definitely not in their terms of reference. The interest in understanding what was happening was very recent. Not knowing the local language was of course another constraint. Korea had a wealth of publications in all the world languages. But these books had rather a "public relations" purpose and are part of the official propaganda.

In addition, the authorities have a well-established practice of communicating strictly what they think the foreigner needed to know for his work. To say the least, they were really not very communicative. For ideological reasons, they considered the floods and droughts as a unique event which forced them to call for outside assistance. The idea of some long-term presence in the form of development cooperation was new and not officially accepted. Reform was never a topic of discussion with foreigners. It was rather a no go. The Koreans would never admit accepting and following foreign advice. But there are a lot of good examples which show that they were listening very carefully.

The official rule was to make the system more efficient but not to question it. The practice showed however that changes were introduced which were not covered by the official rules.

Vantage point, one of the best sources in South Korea of information on the North, lists the most important innovations introduced by the Government.[18]

.

- The constitution of 1998 accepts the right of private trading and mentions explicitly side line activities and the house gardens of the cooperative farms.
- The constitution introduces such notions as well as production costs, prices and profit. The text acknowledges the fact that

---

[18] See Vantage Point, May 2002

prices may change according to demand and quality of the product.

- A clear difference is made between heavy industry, under the authority of the central state, and light industry and agriculture falling into the domain of the local administration (counties).
- The fiscal ratio between central government and the decentralized unit has gradually

  changed. 40% of the budgets are managed by the cities and counties. The composition of the revenue of the central state has changed drastically in favour of profits from state owned companies (1994 20% - 2001 77%)
- The cooperative farms have obtained more autonomy in the new constitution. They are responsible for the cropping pattern on their farms.
- Large companies have been restructured in order to be more flexible in entering into business relations with foreign companies.

These constitutional amendments have been very far reaching. However, they were not directly visible to foreign observers. [19]

Vantage Point concludes its analysis as follows: a conspicuous change is expected to take place in North Korea.

---

[19] Discussing with farm managers later on it became clear how important the market has become for them. However, there were other farm managers who did not even know about these openings.

2. From Emergency Aid to Development Cooperation

2.1. Another Perspective

The (Swiss) Window of Opportunities

One might pose the question about the relevance of the nationality of the author. The answer given would be different according the position of the questioning person. The Swiss would certainly mention the fact that they hosted the 1954 Korean conference in Geneva and since then have been members of the Neutral Nations Supervisory Commission (NNSC) in Panmunjom. This view would probably not be shared by the North Korean government. They considered the Geneva conference unsatisfactory and still think the problem of the Korean Peninsula and the fate of the Korean Nation was not solved in Geneva.

The fact is that the Swiss have been enjoying some special status in North Korea. This might not be felt at government and diplomatic level but it has a strong imprint on the daily working relations. For the external observer, it is noteworthy that the Swiss in North Korea have had access to provinces where no UN agency has so far been able to enter.[20] While the donors were complaining about insufficient coordination among the ministries and the lack of communication, the Swiss could organise inter-ministerial workshops, thus promoting the horizontal flow of information, which is thought impossible in the vertical command channel of the "stone age" communist country.

---

[20] e.g. the region of Pujon.

The Swiss managed to venture into cooperation with technical ministries such as the Ministry of Land and Environment, with the aim of making sloping land agriculture more sustainable. This in a situation where sloping land agriculture did not exist in the government terminology. Switzerland had been organising training courses for North Korean diplomats in Geneva for years, organised fact-finding missions in other Asian countries, and finally launched a business school in Pyongyang teaching open market practices and the importance of free exchange.

The reason for the special standing of the Swiss in North Korea is complicated and, to a certain degree, also contradictory. Isn't Switzerland the model of a capitalist free market economy with strong democratic structures, and in fact just the contrary of North Korea? I see three different lines of argument explaining the special status of the Swiss. Each of them is somehow interrelated:

1. Since the Geneva Conference, DPRK has had in Geneva the largest diplomatic mission in the west. Virtually all diplomats on mission somehow travelled through Geneva, to the point that the embassy has even rented dormitories for their diplomats to stay in. They cash the per diem paid by international organisations and hand this money over to the embassy. Instead of five stars, they stay in dormitories. The Embassy in Geneva actually represents the country in UN organisations. The official Embassy in Switzerland is in a peripheral area in the suburbs of Berne. The villa is usually empty. You have to make a previous appointment if you require a visa. Often you can enjoy the smell of Korean Kimchi in the corridors. The Embassy in Geneva seems to also have a special mission to manage the funds of the ruling family (which are however not dealt with by a major Swiss Bank). The Ambassador has chosen a real Swiss compromise for his residence. He lives neither in Geneva nor in Berne, but somewhere in between.

2. The second reason is the personality of a previous long-time Ambassador to Switzerland. He was probably the most senior head of mission in Switzerland in terms of years of service. He was apparently a close relative of Kim Jong Il. Rumours saw in him a half-brother of the ruler. He played an important role as the mentor of the present leader (and has been serving so far as his foreign minister) The Ambassador was fond of hiking and discovering Switzerland. He was highly knowledgeable about its geography, culture and political system. Whatever he saw on his excursions, he wanted to have copied for his country if it seemed at all appropriate. He was a real genius in mobilizing Swiss resources for his country. He had also the necessary financial means and the leverage to organise visas for specialists he deemed important. The ambassador managed to connect with the association of rabbit breeders, who helped to share their experience with Koreans. He also brought knowhow for fish breeding and backyard chicken keeping to North Korea and helped to contribute to food security and the daily diet of Korean families through bath tub and summer terrace cultivation.

   Probably his master piece was the introduction to Korea of the Saanen goat, a very well-performing Swiss breed. He convinced a rather conservative Swiss Christian church to make a contribution for the starving Korean population. The goats became a real hit in North Korea. They were regularly featured on TV. Actually, they were used to exploit the last ecological reserves very near watersheds. Goat products, mainly in the form of yoghurt, became the absolute runner among the Korean ruling classes. Even the very privileged expats had no access to such products. Naughty tongues suggested that the goat products were mainly sold to the South.

3. Probably a third reason for the special status of the Swiss was the fact that they were early birds in providing assistance when drought and floods hit the country. The Swiss had the

cleverness to provide humanitarian assistance not just through food aid. They brought potato and maize seeds. Knowingly or unknowingly, they probably made the most significant contribution to overcome the food shortage. The Korean agronomists were quick to absorb the new potato technology and reached impressive yields per hectare. Potato growing became so successful that the government made out of Daehongdan a potato growing province. There, the cooperatives were provided with the most advanced equipment by the government. The new potato flood in the north did not change the diet of the population. They did not become potato eaters. They were only interested in the starch for noodle making. The government was very quick in setting up a starch factory built on a turnkey basis by an international company![21] The first agronomists coming back from their educational tour in Vietnam reported a much higher starch output of sweet potatoes.

Less spectacular but more significant was the introduction of new maize varieties. During the 60s the Swiss had developed seeds for maize production in mountain valleys. The vegetation period was substantially shortened. For North Korea, the reduction of the time between plantation and harvest from 105 to 90 days meant that maize could be grown at a higher altitude on slopes with shorter summers. In other words, growing maize on the slopes became a new window of opportunity, with a number of advantages: the slopes did not belong to the responsibility of the Ministry of Agriculture. They were considered forest land, for which the Ministry of Land and Environment was responsible.

---

[21]The factory very soon run into marketing problems because for the Chinese the starch had not sufficient quality and the Swiss potato seeds were never meant for starch production. The yield was below the standard so that the factory could not break even.

Therefore, the production of the slopes was not registered as food to be distributed by the state and it did not appear in the regular reports of WFP/FAO reporting on the hunger situation. The farmers could dispose of this production at their will and did not hesitate to divert fertilizer from the farms to this crop.

The slopes though environmentally under high pressure because of the extractive effect of maize on the soil, became an interesting phenomenon largely ignored by the international experts. I personally met retired men and industrial workers without a job tilling slopes in order to increase their self-sufficiency. I was not aware of any government policy promoting or accepting this production. The benign neglect by the authorities was sufficient.

I do not want to create the impression of being the only Swiss in North Korea. Sometimes I got the impression of that I was experiencing a real Swiss invasion of the country. One of the longest presences was the representative of ABB, probably the only transnational company present permanently in the country. ABB had got - thanks to the good relations between the CEO of ABB and Al Rumsfeld, the later Secretary of Defence of the US government, a contract for the construction of a hydrogen nuclear plant in the framework of the Korea Peninsula Energy Development Agreement (KEDO)[22]. A Swiss national resided in one of the nicest villas of Pyongyang from 2000 onwards. As the construction of the plant was continuously delayed for political, technical and tactical reasons, ABB started to think about the costs of having an expensive

---

[22] Actually, Rumsfeld never admitted any involvement in the awarding of the contract to ABB. But he was the only American sitting on the board of ABB from 1990-2001. According to a CNN report of 2003 he had close contact with the head of the nuclear program of ABB. Percy Barnevik, the then CEO of ABB told me personally in Afghanistan of his personal friendship with Rumsfeld.

representative in the country. [23]He was replaced by another Swiss national, with a kind of part-time assignment. The new man had extensive experience in South East Asia and was married to a Vietnamese. He quickly connected with the business community and started the production of generic drugs in the country. In addition, he helped to organise production chains for ostrich meat, which were produced industrially in a number of cooperatives.

Another very resourceful person was a Swiss lady representing CARITAS Hong Kong. When I was in Pyongyang, she was just celebrating her 10th visit to the country. She looked after children's homes and orphanages. CARITAS Hong Kong was used as an entry point to channel international funds, particularly from South Korean Christians to North Korea. As a long-term visitor, she had an excellent network in the country and whenever we met for dinner in town with or without our Korean colleagues she used to be among us. The Koreans let her work and we were always under the impression that the government was very happy to leave the orphanages to CARITAS in order to be able to show the world how inhumanly the poor Koreans were treated otherwise by the international boycott.

A particular role was played by ADRA (Adventist Development and Relief Agency) Switzerland. They had a lot of cash from ADRA US which passed through Swiss channels. In North Korea, they were active particularly in setting up a large bakery for the general public. As their representative, besides being a convinced Christian and certainly an excellent expert in the processing of wheat flour, had no particular motivation to understand the Korean system, he regularly ran into communication problems with his liaison officer. I was confronted with the phenomenon when relaxed evenings in the SDC residence were sometimes disturbed by urgent needs for mediation.

---

[23] KEDO cancelled formally the construction of the light water reactors on 31st May 2003.

After my arrival, the potato and maize operations had already reached their cruising speeds and did not require further support from SDC. Yet the government had set up some maize seed multiplication farms and imported equipment for the grading and processing of the seeds. The Ambassador in Switzerland apparently managed to mobilize two experts - father and son - for the job. There were other spontaneous visits, which I was certainly not aware of for example the SDC office was once visited by two Swiss gentlemen (again father and son!). Apparently, the ambassador, in one of his outings in the Swiss mountains, met on a construction site these two guys installing a new type of heating. The Ambassador invited them immediately to Korea in order to build the same system there. (We did not quite understand the rationale for this transfer as we were rather impressed by the efficiency of heating in the traditional Korean houses. We rather saw the potential to learn from Korean technology).

The goat project was becoming so popular and well known in North Korea that even UNDP wanted to launch a goat project under the flag of "innovative projects"! I was asked

to explore the market of Swiss suppliers for goat cheese processing equipment during a home-leave. After I was able to identify the three most important suppliers, I tried to introduce the potential of the Korean market to them. As a matter of fact, no company produced exclusively equipment for goat cheese, but on the other hand, there were knowledgeable persons. The contact with these companies proved to me that I was an utterly naïve person. The first told me that their expert was just on mission in DPRK, the second said they were in contact with the embassy to send a load of cheese making equipment to DPRK and the third mentioned they had in the past regularly sent equipment to DKRK and they could tell me what equipment was listed traditionally.

Within the multifaceted presence of "Swissness" belonged certainly the head of the evaluation of WFP[24] and the CTA of the only ongoing FAO/UNDP project, a Peruvian of Swiss descent.

The Unexpected Boosters

I do not remember exactly why I was selected as a mission member for the fact-finding mission to explore the chances to use the momentum of the sunshine policy for enhanced development cooperation and an integration of DPRK into the global community of nations. Above all, I tried to explore the reasons for choosing a Swiss. Probably I was just the only consultant available.

For me, the association with a team exploring the possibilities of helping North Korea out of its isolation was highly challenging. The association with change, or what we thought could be a change in DPRK was not only professionally but also personally a profound experience. I think also that I benefited from very positive framework conditions and the support of and influence from specific personalities. They made my Korean experience very particular and made me think it might be worthwhile writing it down.

So before entering materially into the subject, let me try to explain why I think I managed to exploit a certain momentum designed by others. I have to insist on this point. The concrete situation proved that human relations are a key for progress and in advancing a cause. Of course, DPRK was known as one of the most ruthless countries with a very harsh way in dealing with individuals who refused the rigidity of the system.

---

[24] Actually, Pyongyang rumours gave him an American passport. His Swissness was just a good appearance. His wife was the operations officer of UNDP. She was in charge of controlling the appropriate use of funds, an issue questioned by the American government later on.

But it is also true that the country is part of Asia. It shares some of that continent's key characteristics: namely that human relations manage to mitigate the rules of the game imposed by the system.

I think that three persons particularly helped to make my assignment a very satisfying experience.

1. The first was my partner, supervisor and/or controller from the Foreign Ministry. He was a senior advisor in charge of the multilateral organisations. He was officially called "coordinator". Let us call him "supervisor". This is what might have been written in his terms of reference. In reality, he was more a colleague. I could not call him a friend. Our relationship was too much influenced by the fact that each of us tried to draw as much information as possible from the other and both were clearly determined to tell the other what one thought the other should know in order to make him say what the other wanted to know. My supervisor looked rather grim and was always very serious. At first sight, he belonged to the stereotype of a communist party functionary. At second sight, he was a very pragmatic and problem- solving oriented person. Arriving in Pyongyang, I never went with him to pay respects to the statue of the Great Leader as was the practice of foreign visitors. When I wondered about this, his swift reaction was that I was no visitor and had work to be done. We connected fairly well. Maybe this was also due to the fact that he had a long period of working in the Embassy in Geneva, where his daughter attended a public school. There he apparently developed a liking for red wine. A typical scenario would be as follows: he would meet me at the airport and inform me where I could at present buy the best red wine in town (usually in a shop owned by an

Argentinian(!). So before going to the guesthouse, we pur-
chased a box of red wine.

My supervisor never interfered in my work. In the evening, he came to fetch me in my office in the UN compound
and brought me to our common guesthouse. However, we
were allowed to eat together only if we had some official
reason, which we organised once a week. The usual
rhythm was that before dinner, we were sitting – only the
two of us - at the bar of the guesthouse and drank a bottle
of red wine. Unavoidably we had to talk about something
on such occasions. These aperitif sessions gradually became for me the highlight of the day. I learnt a lot about
the thinking and what I felt was the Korean's logic of arguing. When we had emptied our bottle, we also dealt with
topics not belonging exactly on our duty sheets. My drinking colleague was fairly clever. He remained very purpose-
ful in what he was telling me. He knew what he wanted
me to know. For me the art was to entice him to go beyond and have him tell me what I wanted to know. I do
not know who was winning these ping-pong games.

2. The second person who stood like a pillar in my DPRK ex-
    perience was the representative of the Swiss Develop-
    ment Cooperation(SDC) in Pyongyang. As a matter of fact,
    I wore two hats in DPRK. I was a Chief Technical Advisor
    (CTA) to UNDP. In parallel, SDC made me a strategic advi-
    sor for the development of their programme. (the term
    "strategic" was probably chosen to get a higher consult-
    ant's fee). So, the representative became my second su-
    pervisor, partner and friend. While his predecessors were
    formally part of the humanitarian assistance breed, my
    new boss was the first person representing long-term de-
    velopment cooperation. This man was quite a character. I
    always teased him as being a typical representative of his

tribe from the Swiss Hinterland, the Emmental. His appearance was always reserved, rather timid. Towards outsiders he was highly respectful and certainly never offensive. He was a personality you tended to underestimate. His non-imposing appearance hid a highly intelligent and very determined personality with a clear vision.

This kind of personality apparently went well with the Korean psyche. They held him in high esteem and he got very positive reactions (and often also solutions which did not follow the text book). He had an outstanding ability to learn foreign languages. During his previous assignment in Kirgizstan he had learnt Russian, which proved now to be an unexpected advantage. Westerners were not supposed to learn Korean and their contact with the locals was not encouraged, to say the least. This was different for the former communist allies. Somehow, they had a different status in Korean society, and this had not changed with the end of the Cold War. Our man got a Korean teacher using Russian as a means of communication. This elderly lady proved to be an invaluable source of information on history, local customs and also politics. She helped an unofficial narrative to flow into the perception of the Swiss delegation.

The Koreans reacted with amazement that a westerner spoke in the local language. To get an idea of the effect, let me mention one crucial experience: the head of the SDC office invited his staff monthly for a social evening. Good food and alcohol were taken for granted. But such evenings ended with songs. A microphone was always very close by, and singing was like balm for the Korean soul.

Now the climax of the evening was reached: the host took the mike and gave a Korean song in Korean. His staff didn't even try to hide their admiration. Even persons from the foreign ministry approached me with amazement and asked why the Swiss should be so kind and understanding.

It was certainly not a coincidence that the atmosphere in the office was relaxed and friendly. For me the most striking consequence was that the liaison officer apparently had the authority to approve travelling in the countryside. While working with UN, I had to communicate my plans always a week ahead and was always accompanied by an official person. Working with SDC, travelling was much easier without any official baggage. I remember we even visited cooperative farms without previous announcement. The social environment and working relationship in the Swiss office could not have been more different from the UN set-up (office and residence of the Swiss was not in the diplomatic enclave. They had taken over the building of the former Hungarian Embassy outside). Working with the Swiss, I could stay at their residence, which was apparently not exactly as foreseen by the authorities.

3. The third anchor of importance for my work was less personal but highly relevant for one of my major area of interest, food scarcity and food security. One of my usual guesthouses belonged, as I later came to know, to the Korean Foreign Insurance Company (KFIC). This company was founded in 1947. The original purpose was to insure Korean marine commerce. The scope gradually widened and is now covering property, marine commerce and agriculture.

One evening I returned from the office with my supervisor. We went to the small bar for our usual red wine sundowner. We exceptionally were not alone. Two foreign gentlemen were already having a drink. To my utter surprise they were talking in Swiss German! Later, during dinner and in Switzerland while following up the contacts I discovered a new world. The two gentlemen represented a Swiss reinsurance intermediary. Their company had been in business relations with KFIC since 1985. For them, their Korean partner was a functional and efficient company working in modern premises with state-of-the art equipment. They dealt with KFIC in the reinsurance of agricultural production, particularly rice and maize. They visited DPRK once or twice a year. In case of insurance claims, they were able to verify the local situation with independent experts and modern means of verification (videos, helicopter flights). The government had set up (at least officially) an independent institution, the Central Agricultural Risk Association (CARA), which was given the task of regularly verifying agricultural production. They had to report to the reinsurance four times a year at specific moments on the crop (seed germination, upcoming crop, standing crop; for maize, they counted the number of stems per square meter, the number of cones per stem and the number of seeds per cone based on a defined sample and before harvest). The contract had clearly defined trigger points for the insurance to kick in. Reporting and business behaviour was judged very reliable and professional by my two Swiss co-nationals.

Apparently, agriculture accounts for about 20% of the turnover of the company. After the floods of 1996 KFIC had to pay huge amounts to the cooperatives and the company would not have survived without loans from the Government which had not yet been reimbursed.

Lately reinsurance has become difficult. For political reasons the big global reinsurance companies have backed out and the intermediary managed to cover not more than 15% of the production.

For me this information was more than an eye-opener. I did not know of any government in the world setting up insurance for the agricultural production against drought, floods and wind. Of course, the fact that there had been an international reinsurance since 1985 was just unbelievable, and nobody knowing or telling about it. In my follow-up, I could peruse the documents and verify certain information.

Now I had factual proof that the reporting of FAO/WFP was not reliable and even definitely wrong. This confirmed our own estimates.

Well, these new realities were not exactly helpful. For reasons of confidentiality I could neither quote the reports nor announce the sources of information. Consequently, my statements were not taken seriously by the humanitarian coordinator of UN, who was a WFP man in DPRK. I suggested WFP to look for contacts with CARA. I also sounded out my supervisor - and got a rare but strong rebuke from him: I should focus on my own assignment, was his answer. The following day he made a speech to me, leaving not a straw of credibility for the KFIC and denied the existence of CARA. This closed the topic in our conversation. Myself I felt confirmed in my pursuance of questioning the hypothesis so dear to the international players of hunger in DPRK.

All this explains why my working relationship in North Korea was influenced by certain coincidences and rather significant framework conditions. My reading and understanding of my environment was strongly shaped by these situations.[25] Maybe the most important one was the

---

[25] The niche for the Swiss disappeared after the Swiss foreign minister was invited to cross the closed frontier between North and South by foot. This step and the visit to North Korea got such wide press coverage in Switzerland that the national- conservatives in the federal Parliament moved a motion asking for the end of development cooperation with NK. The Swiss managed to ruin their special relations with North Korea by forbidding in 2016 the exportation

fact that, as already mentioned above, I was wearing two different hats at the same time:

- I was appointed a member of the joint donor mission team and, against all rules and regulations, became Chief Technical Advisor (CTA). The fact that a mission member of the fact-finding and feasibility mission could be a CTA of an UNDP programme had to be cleared by the legal services of UNDP in New York. I was to spend 18 months of work in three years for the project.
- At the same time, I was consultant for the programme development of SDC. The Swiss government was the first to switch gear from short term humanitarian assistance to long term development cooperation. Actually, the program was not changed substantially, but the bureaucracy needed a new justification. My task was to help to develop a rational framework in this new perspective.

Both assignments were clearly separated but they complemented each other. Especially my UN assignment became much more efficient thanks to the financial and technical support I could mobilize through the bilateral programme. The triangle between the SDC representation in Pyongyang, the headquarters in Berne and myself, worked well. The SDC headquarters proved to be extremely flexible. Thanks to this constellation we managed to generate a significant impact with comparatively few resources.

Finally, I had an advantage: I was a development guy, virtually the shark in a pond of carp, in an environment where expatriate staff was recruited to provide emergency aid. I had the impression I had a com-

---

to NK of a second-hand cable car out of use in Switzerland. They have probably blighted their hopes to play a mediatory role in the Korean conflict.

pletely different way of thinking. I spent also long evenings in Pyong-yang and time in Switzerland reading secondary literature published partly after the opening of the Soviet archives in Moscow, publications of think tanks in South Korea and Korean Publications, of which the works of Kim Il Sung were not exactly amusing but certainly very telling.

2.2. Trying to Push the Door open

The Sunshine Policy creates a new Opening

With the Sunshine Policy initiated by the president of South Korea, Kim Dae Jung, and the establishment of diplomatic relations between 20 European countries and the DPRK, there was widespread optimism that the situation on the Korean Peninsula would stabilize. Among the donors there were intensive consultations including the international NGOs present in the country.

All parties concerned, the international community under the leadership of UN and the government of DPRK, had their own rationale for the initiative. The western players, and these included also the former socialist countries of Eastern Europe, hoped for an opening of the country and a readiness for reform. For them, North Korea was basically a latecomer of change after the end of the Soviet Union and the COMECON. Their reading was that the country was condemned to open up or to end in disaster. Proof for their analysis was that the government was not able to feed its population. The reports produced regularly by special missions of FAO/WFP showed that 6 out of 23 million Koreans went hungry. The support in terms of food aid was strictly and exclusively channelled to the civil population and by no means encouraged the government to go for fundamental reforms. The World Food Programme had set up a huge apparatus to directly control the distribution of food.

The head of the UN mission in the country was exceptionally not a representative of the United Nations Development Programme but a person of WFP.

The position of the Koreans was rather diametrically opposed. For them the country had a highly industrialized standard which did not need change. Their country was boycotted by the international world under the leadership of the United States. Their position was that the boycott had to be ended. Since the armistice 1953 the country remained in a state of war. This status could only be changed through international peace negotiations, which would imply an eye-to-eye negotiation of equal partners, one of them the US.

From the UN, they expected to get access to modern technology and acquire some of the goods they were terribly lac king since the end of the Soviet Union.

In this context, the government consented to invite a mission organised by UN in order to explore the chances of changing the working relationship. A joint donor mission was fielded in 2001. The terminology used for the mission and its tasks was carefully chosen and UN wanted to make sure that all the other stakeholders were on board. The mission was composed of three persons. The head of mission was a former very senior official from Vietnam, who had already participated in various missions in North Korea. His choice was crucial. An important aspect of the first mission was confidence building and he was the man having the confidence of the Koreans and therefore access beyond the formal diplomatic formalities. The second person was of Swedish nationality, working for the UN SURF in Bangkok. The third was myself, a Swiss national. The reason for our appointment at first glance was that Sweden and Switzerland were both members of the international supervisory commission between the two Koreas. However, the justification was more down to earth. At least I had the impression that the Swedish colleague had just a Swedish nationality. He represented the UN and I got the strong feeling his main task was to observe the mission head, in whom the UN had no trust for being too close and familiar with North Korea. The presence of a Swiss was justified due to the early change of the working mode of the Swiss. They were the first and virtually the only ones interpreting humanitarian assistance in a rather broad way and bringing new seeds and technology into the country. In practice, the division of labour among the three worked pretty well. The head of our mission had the necessary access and relations, the Swede had had all of his education in the English system. He was, therefore, supposed to write a text in decent English. He was the born report writer. For myself remained the role of the practical development person.

The mission was titled "Capacity Building for Enhanced Development Cooperation". The purpose was what might be called a fact-finding and confidence building mission. Nobody expected concrete results at this stage. We tried to identify the level of interest of the discussion partners and where they saw constraints and potentials in the cooperation. The expectations on the part of the international organisations, embassies and NGOs were low. They did not put trust in any change. The Korean partners were very cautious. We quickly learned that terms such as reform, structural change, reorganisation or development assistance had to be avoided. They quickly led to an impasse and our Korean partners categorically refused to enter into discussions.

We became aware that government policies could not be questioned. Strategies and visions were no topic of interest. For our partners, the principles of Marxism and Leninism had to be followed. There was no need for additional strategies. Within the mission the conclusion was that macro-policies such as reforms, reorganisation, taxes, import- export, budgets and so on had to be avoided. We had to limit ourselves to what we called the meso level: sectorial programmes, capacity building of personnel and project management. Verifying this hypothesis, we realized that even the term "project" was not really understood by the partners.

Based on the positive reactions and a scrutiny of the report, UN and the Korean government decided to take the initiative to the next level and organise a second mission. The overall objective of this mission was to design, in consultation with the Government and donors, a project document on "Capacity Building for Enhanced Development Co-operation", based on the key outcomes and related activities suggested in August 2001 by the Joint Mission.

Assuming that the project would get a positive response, its role was to create the environment for the donors to switch from humanitarian assistance to development cooperation and prepare the documents for a Round Table Meeting between the North Korean government and the donors.

The mission prepared terms of reference for the CTA who was supposed to lead the process. To my surprise, the Koreans proposed me as CTA. Making a member of the fact-finding and the planning mission CTA of the project was not only unusual, it was not in line with UN rules and regulations. Somehow an exception was granted and I was nominated CTA. This was also the expression of the urgency certain participants felt. In September, the Prime Minister of Japan, Koizumi, visited DPRK. It was a visit combined with high expectations. The Prime Minister had excused Japan for the atrocities committed during the colonial period. The Koreans expected substantial compensation payments. During the visit, Kim Yong Il admitted that DPRK had abducted 11 Japanese nationals and brought them to North Korea. When the Prime Minister returned home with this information he ran into a heavy storm of public opinion. The idea of paying compensation to DPRK was considered politically and ethically impossible. In North Korea, the hope of access to new resources and the belief in a changing attitude of the donors diminished substantially.

Coordination and Access to Data

The availability of basic information and data as well as the regular consultation between the government and the donors is a prerequisite for development cooperation.

After 1996 the government had created an official partner institution for the coordination of all emergency assistance, the FDRC (Flood Disaster Rehabilitation Committee) which deputed liaison officers to all agencies and basically made available also the local personnel required by the donors.

The communication was usually a one-way channel. The periodic written progress reports and the liaison officers were the only contacts with the Government. The foreign agencies on their part had regular exchange and discussions among themselves.

Up to 2000 this communication pattern had not changed. The institutional behaviour was shaped by the urgency of reducing hunger. There was no need for in-depth analysis. The foreign agencies wanted to bring quick and efficient relief. The tasks of the Korean partners were to show how needy the country was.

After 2000 the situation had changed. Even if everybody was talking of relief and urgency (and reporting to FDRC – only the Swiss reported to the Ministry of Foreign Affairs), in reality the attitude had changed: South Korea, Japan and the United States provided fertilizer, petrol and food aid as part of the KEDO arrangement (a compensation for DPRK to discontinue the development of the nuclear capacity) The European Union provided fertilizer to cooperatives in the surroundings of the capital. Their window for short term emergency, ECHO, financed on a regular basis four European NGOs for the rehabilitation and development work. The administrative functioning remained still in the emergency mode: one year contracts, which could be extended to 15 months. The three months extension periods were used to prepare the next phase of twelve months. In other words, the practical work just remained with the term of relief. In reality they had switched to a rehabilitation and even development mode. The approach of other agencies and the UN was similar: e.g. UNICEF provided rural water supply and child and mother care as in any other country but called it emergency aid in DPRK.

The change into development mode meant that their need for data and contact with technical ministries were essential in order to put their work on a solid base.

The Programme for the enhancement of development cooperation should now help to prepare the administration for development cooperation and convince the donors to make longer term commitments aiming at rehabilitation and sustainable development. The government, according to the project document, was to set up a project coordination unit with a national coordinator and a steering committee composed of the most important players on the government side. This change, considered by the donors as a prerequisite for the intensification of the cooperation, proved to be much more difficult than we had imagined.

- The national coordinator was never formally nominated. In reality, the UN coordinator, my supervisor, took over this function.
- The Project unit with its own personnel and administration was never created.
- The steering committee did timidly take informal shape in the form of a few meetings. These get-togethers were not more than a platform for exchange of information. The sources of information were exclusively the foreign partners.

The sobering beginning led to a soul-searching exercise. The project management drew the following conclusions:

- The Ministry of Foreign Affairs, the Division for multilateral organisations, had the lead for the exercise. But the

leverage to invite and convince the technical ministries did not exist.
- The FDRC had not the slightest interest in having their responsibilities diminished. They wanted to save their domain and their power and did everything not to give up any of their prerogatives.
- There was an absence of political will within the Government to change the operation mode from emergency to long-term cooperation. The authorities let us do so, and observed what happened, but did nothing to make it happen.
- There was a very practical reason. Most of the ministries had no capacity to communicate with foreign agencies. This was partly an issue of administrative authority. Corresponding units were required within the ministries. There was also the simple problem that the officers had language problems and were scared to communicate with foreigners. Wearing my hat as a bilateral Swiss consultant I observed how the communication became gradually much easier with the creation of a foreign department. Apparently, we, the foreigners, had been too impatient.

My reading during the long and cold evenings in my guesthouse made me also aware of a very fundamental problem. My source of information was among others the works of Kim Il Sung. These publications could be bought in any bookshop in all languages you could imagine. The collection had reached some 25 or 30 volumes. These books are mainly a collection of speeches of the Great Leader. There, you find information you would expect in a parliamentary democracy in the collection of laws and the proceedings of parliament. The books give in extenso the speeches of the Leader at official occasions. Very instructive were his visits to cooperatives. While reading these very lengthy and boring speeches, which were certainly meant to be educational, you could find out the real problems in putting the socialist ideals into practice. Here, I became aware also that the Koreans were simply not in a position to provide information and data useful for the planning of development cooperation.

Of course, the Korean bureaucracy produced an unprecedented amount of information and reports. They were collected and composed using quite different reasoning than we expected. Their reporting responded to a purely administrative and partly political/ideological purpose. The ideas were not to relate input with output, to reach a certain target with efficiency, or to have an impact or to be effective in reaching an operational target. Reporting was very much influenced by the need to reach an objective set forward for political and ideological reasons and you got rewarded if you satisfied these criteria. On his tours through the country, the Great Leader realised that the targets achieved in the reports did not necessarily reflect the reality in the field but corresponded rather with the figures a certain crop could reach in a research station. Ever recurring problems were the postharvest losses, the non-availability of equipment, the lacking storing space etc. The result reported depended very much on whether the data were taken from the field, at the farm's gate or the amount ceded to the government distribution system. The system pushes you to report so that you appear in the best possible light in the eyes of the superior. If disastrous mistakes are discovered, then your socialist education has to be improved.

My interpretation was that the Koreans were aware that the reports and data therein did not always correspond with realities but nobody wanted to expose themselves. Especially when we introduced the topic of food security, we quickly realised that there was another dimension of information provision. The Koreans were very shrewd and used information very purposefully. They provided exactly the amount of information in terms of quality and quantity they required for a negotiation. Interpreting information and ascertaining its value always implied that you tried to understand what your partner wanted to achieve with the information.

Capacity Development and Training

For the definition of the potential and constraints for capacity development we had to reassess our entry point. We had to bridge the gap between the point of view of the foreign agencies, which clearly stated that no change from emergency to development cooperation was possible without a change of the system with reforms, and a changing attitude towards foreign inputs. The Korean government, which categorically refused any questioning of the system, was expected to have a more forthcoming communication.

This meant that we had to overcome a basic scepticism and distrust, which was not just directed against the "capitalist" foreigners but against foreigners in general. Our first effort was to try to make clear some basic principles in development cooperation. We needed to create a basic understanding of the mechanism of international and bilateral organisations.

- Presentation of the international development setup
- Explanation of the terminology
- Showing the internal functioning of the agencies
- Showing the different instruments
- Giving a rational for the need for an exchange of information and experiences and the need of basic data etc.

The programme management felt under pressure in a context of anxiety and high expectations at the same time. The international agencies on the one hand observed our dealings very closely and with a strong dose of pessimism. On the other hand, they expected us to prepare a Round Table Meeting between Donors and the government. Such a meeting, serving as an opening for long term development cooperation, had to be prepared by solid reports with facts and figures. The capacity development therefore had to produce quick results for the next step with full cooperation from the Korean side.

However, the first challenge was on our side. We had to find consultants familiar with the special situation, acceptable to the Korean authorities and ready to work in North Korea. The natural source for the recruitment was the regional UN office in Bangkok. They had set up a new organisational unit called SURF which was a kind of clearinghouse and intermediary for international knowhow. In reality, this hub was only of very limited use. The Korean government refused to accept more than US $ 500.- payment a day for a UNDP consultant and the hub under this condition could only mobilize consultants from their preferred retirement in Chien Mai in Northern Thailand. These candidates again were not acceptable to the Koreans. I didn't see another way out but using funds from the Swiss contribution and looking for Swiss candidates. This proved rather difficult and required a lot of persuasion. The consultants had problems to imagine working in a country like North Korea, and promoting development cooperation in the "stone-age communist "country seemed unfeasible.

In a first phase, we wanted to promote a layer of persons in the institutions who understood development cooperation. We were aiming at two target groups: the liaison officers with the foreign agencies, and government officials who were close to existing or potentially new programmes.

The capacity building events with the liaison officers did not work out well. The atmosphere was not very congenial from the very beginning and the third course was cancelled. The liaison officers were reporting to the FDRC and this committee had absolutely no interest in the officers being trained in subjects which potentially threw the committee out of the market.

The sessions with the officers from the ministries were much more positive. The participants were motivated and interested. Their responsiveness could not hide a fundamental difficulty. The courses were given in English, spontaneously translated by professional interpreters. The issue was that the technical terms had never been translated into the Korean language. This meant that in fact new terms had to be created and agreed upon, a task which went beyond simple translation. Unfortunately, we had no competent partner on the Korean side who could have helped us. Teachers and learners had to create a new understanding, which at the end proved of limited value. Within their institutions the officers had to talk to their superiors in a language understood by them. So we had to question our starting hypotheses, namely to work at meso level addressing procedures and the functioning of development cooperation. Even very motivated participants got frustrated. The training helped them to communicate with the foreigners but made it difficult to bring the messages home to their ministries.

Using Loopholes as a Strategy

Wearing my second hat as consultant of Swiss Development Cooperation (SDC), my task was to support the local SDC office for the preparation of a special Korean Programme. SDC had decided, as part of the opening following the sunshine policy, to convert their actions officially into a development cooperation programme. Practically it was a change of terminology. The projects supported with the provision of improved potato and maize seeds and supporting the raising of small animals were already part of the programme. The main challenge for the consultant was to redefine the rationale for long-term cooperation mainly for internal administrative reasons in the Swiss administration. New aspects were included based on the ongoing experience.

This ongoing programme included Sustainable Agricultural Production and Agro Processing and Market Development, focussing on thematic issues that combined continuity and innovation in a way that permitted building on past experience and at the same time shifting towards relevant and pressing challenges of the presently evolving context.

The third component, **Capacity Development**, was considered a transversal theme. This approach, formulated by SDC in a concept paper, was to be applied in a more systematic way in the projects.

Reform and opening were in 2001 and 2002 the buzz words in the discussions of the international community. We were actively interpreting any statement by official authorities as well the gestures in everyday life. The opening of a business school was an excellent example: a Pyongyang Business School had been discussed with the authorities for half a year. The immediate partners had the greatest interest but did not hide their apprehension. The file seemed to be blocked somewhere. After one year, all of a sudden, everything seemed possible and with the third session the interest was so great that not all the applicants could be considered. The authority to accept and refuse lay apparently with the SDC liaison officer, who solved the problem of high attendance in accepting for every session other candidates, which evidently did not go down well with the teachers.

We had the impression that with the persons we had daily contacts with, a certain liberalism was enjoyed, which however was not confirmed by the institutional behaviour. We observed a growing criticism of the international NGO. The government was of the opinion that their representatives were travelling too much and their contribution was not evident. Another experience was the already mentioned Project Cycle Management courses. With each session, they seemed to get more positive echos and feedbacks from the participants and representatives of the government. But officially there was no statement and no nomination of a counterpart. We definitely had the feeling the Government was not convinced of the usefulness of these courses - but they let them take place. It was a similar attitude within other innovations which were clearly part of a reform agenda. The authorities somehow let them happen and observed the consequences. Thus, we were under the impression that a lot of new things were possible, but we missed an official sanction.

Our optimism was not shared by everybody. The donors expected clear declarations of the Government and were not happy with the pragmatism we enjoyed the operational level. From the Swiss side, the training course of diplomats in Geneva was being questioned.

Sloping land management along with the Business School were the two new hits of the programme. Both had the potential to play a very substantial role in the future development of the country provided the cooperation was proceeding with care. We considered the involvement in sloping land management as absolutely strategic. The justification was difficult for outsiders because of the missing data and the fact that something like sloping land agriculture did not exist.

Administratively speaking the above-mentioned 2'000'000 ha agricultural land were split into about 3'500 cooperatives and seed farms. They were formally the responsibility of the Ministry of Agriculture. The sloping land is part of the domain of the Ministry of Land Protection and Environment. It is supposed to be covered by forest and the ministry responsible has the mandate to afforest the slopes. (The economically extractable forest is part of the Ministry of Forestry, which as in the case of Agriculture has the task to extract and manage the resources.)

Sloping land in a strict legal sense is not open for agricultural production. The crisis of the 90s has however led widely to encroachment. Sloping land is being used by the strongly promoted goat population and by people who produce for their own consumption. As this cultivation is not official there are no reliable reports and the yields are not recorded and included in any official figures. Assuming very conservatively yields of 1 ton per ha the production could be close to the officially declared food deficit. The communicated position of the government is that old and jobless people are allowed to use the sloping land in a period of scarcity.

The SDC office took up contact with the ministry as early as 2002 in order to investigate the interest in cooperation. We certainly had a lucky stroke once again. This ministry either already had a foreign department, or at least a man in charge who spoke even French. The second stroke was our consultant: a soft spoken but very experienced forester who managed to connect well with the national colleagues. First SDC organised an exposure trip to South East Asian countries and a workshop in DPRK. Based on these findings a first pilot project was implemented on three plots in Suan County, an area belonging to the Miru Hill area. The first experiences have proved very promising and constituted a basis for a longer-term programme. I had the chance of assisting at one of the workshops. The first innovation was that three different ministries sent their representatives. The Korean administration was strictly organised into what we called silos, in other words, strictly top-down with no spill overs right or left. Horizontal exchange was highly unusual and not encouraged. The second aspect was the friendly subject matter discussion among the participants. What helped was that some senior persons had already worked in Africa as part of the DPRK aid programme during the 80s. For me, an absolute eye opener were the field visits. We could visit the slopes, talk to the persons working there and discover a new world: the persons working were either retired or factory workers. They were only exceptionally from an agricultural farm. They took the interaction with the visitors as a good change and I didn't feel any difference compared with an African or South Asian country.

Meeting Industrial workers in Suan District working on sloping Agriculture

The lack of figures though was a serious setback for the justification of a new programme. So we took a lot of pictures and made an effort to argue qualitatively. Cooperation in sloping land management responds to a number of substantial challenges, each justifying cooperation in its own right.

-   The sloping land is ecologically fragile and requires sustainable management methods. This means the practice of agro forestry. i.e. the planting of trees along contour lines with sustainable production methods. For the government, this is a step towards the reconstitution of the slopes as non-agricultural land in the long run.

- The families working on the slopes belong to the poor and vulnerable. Working on slopes signifies a substantial contribution to food security in a critical environment.
- The production is not part of the central planning figures. The produce may be sold or consumed by the users themselves. This increases the niche for flexibility and local marketing.
- The fact that SDC is cooperating with the ministry and supports the individuals in getting organised in groups brings institutional stability by converting a quasi-illegal activity into an officially recognised one.

Strategically speaking we were of the opinion that we were making a substantial contribution not only to food security but to the autonomy of people and the weakening of the central distribution system of the government. This actually was an overriding justification for our endeavour.

Workshop on sloping Land agriculture with representatives of the Ministries of Agriculture and Land and Environment

Hope for Change

Already after the Project planning mission, but particularly after the visit of the Japanese Prime Minister Koizumi, the political frame condition had changed. The hope for a political breakthrough had diminished and optimism was replaced by a sobering realism. Nevertheless, we thought we had generally a good response from the authorities and saw signs for openness. We were of the opinion that in spite of the negative geopolitical signs, our mission was on track. We were under the impression that the harsh official discourse of the Koreans was hiding the conviction that they had to move against all odds.

Every statement and gesture from authorities and the way my supervisor reacted was scrutinized with the hope of detecting traces of flexibility. This behaviour had a strong imprint on daily life.

During the first missions, in the rare restaurants we could visit, we were flooded by nationalist, almost military-like march music. Apparently, they wanted to make sure that we were aware of the socialist model country we were visiting. All of a sudden, these restaurants discovered American soundtracks and hits of the 70s (never jazz however, which was considered as second-class negro music). The number of places to go increased and the managers were often so-called Japanese Koreans, Koreans who had come back from Japan. The inhabitants of an apartment block were authorized to open restaurants on the ground floor. They often had real menu cards. We observed also little selling spots close to the entrance of such buildings, where women sold cookies and other products prepared in their households. We had also an insight into increasing off-farm activities of the cooperatives. People were talking about farmer markets though I never saw one. Either I was too well protected - or what I suspected - these were very informal arrangements. The farmers knew exactly how much rice they could get from other cooperatives for a certain quantity of seed potatoes.

It was quite impossible to ignore the national TV during the meals. Besides the very short English news, we could follow the pictures of interesting features. Besides the dramatic voices of political propaganda, the TV was apparently serving educational purposes. The daily features were on raising small livestock (rabbits and chicken), feeding Tilapia fish in ponds and, never ending, on keeping goats. We cracked jokes about the hobby of the dear leader to keep his people amused with unrealistic hobbies when the TV projected stories of ostrich keeping and praised their meat, until my colleague from ABB who had by now muted into a business consultant, explained to me that he was advising some cooperatives for the import of equipment for a production chain for ostrich butchering. It became evident that the government encouraged the inhabitants to diversify their sources of food and to develop initiatives for a production which extended beyond the family circle and was also not included in statistics in the public distribution system.

Early morning before breakfast I used to take my personal exercise in the form of jogging. Behind the guesthouse of the insurance company was an extended forest with nice viewpoints and pleasant footpaths. Even at daybreak and during the harshest winter days I usually met people there. One of my routine encounters was a group of about 20 retired persons, women and men, who did their early morning outing in the form of some physical exercises which reminded me of the early morning exercises proposed by a veteran sports king on the Swiss radio, when I was a youngster. These encounters became a kind of tradition. They greeted me with "dobre utra" to which I responded in the same way. From a certain moment, I thought I had to show that I was not Russian and the country was opening up. So, I greeted them now with "good morning" and I got a reply: "god morning" in a clear accent. I pushed my exercise further and switched to "Guten Morgen" and got a perfect "Guten Morgen" back. Now I felt a challenge and switched to a "Grüessech", the way we do in the Swiss mountains. I was probably too exhausted and do not remember whether I got an answer. On my early morning jogging I used to meet "by coincidence" my supervisor in a thick overall and fur cap. When I innocently asked him whether he liked this kind of early morning exercise, he told me he had to protect me against unfriendly encounters because this was a military protected area. As a consultant of SDC I stayed the night in the Swiss compound, which was too far away from the forest, so I jogged following the river. I was never stopped or interviewed. In a meeting in the foreign ministry one of the persons present teased me as an early morning jogger in places I should not be. Apparently, they were perfectly informed.

I had a particular encounter with my supervisor in Switzerland. I knew he was attending an UNCTAD conference in Geneva. So, I invited him to my house. I took for granted that he would arrive by train and wanted to meet him at a given hour on the platform of the railway station. As he had not shown up I realised he had arrived on the other side of the railway station in a black Mercedes car. I was aware that the practice was that a Korean abroad was never alone. But there were four of them! One was wearing a lose T-shirt and shorts, the second was a quiet serious man, plus the driver and my supervisor. The person in shorts behaved and talked like an American. He was working in the University of California, the   second was a Korean Professor from Japan. They were in Geneva to help the North Korean delegation to formulate and defend their position at the UN conference. The young person explained to me that he was a second-generation Korean from Japan. His family came from the north and his father has always been a socialist. They consider DPRK as their home and in Japan they had a strong community. I took the group for sightseeing to the Schilthorn and the Trümmelbach Fälle and was a little disappointed that they did not voice any enthusiasm for the views of the snow mountains and the natural water mills in the rocks. My supervisor commented only drily, that the steps climbing to the water falls were not yet made out of concrete five years ago…Apparently, the visit was not new to them!

While on mission in Korea, the supervisor always had the impression he had to keep me and   consultants busy. We often played snooker (the Koreans as experts, myself as a pitiful beginner), played badminton with old wooden tennis rackets or even went for a hike. A highlight was going to the seaside for swimming and playing volleyball on the sand. It happened that all of a sudden, an enigmatic diver with a rusty boat and archaic diving gear appeared and brought us mussels for the evening. They were spread on the soil and then cooked by being sprinkled with fuel the drivers took from the tanks of their cars and then burned.

I remember once we agreed to go to a shooting range, which had been built for some world meeting of socialist youth. I thought for once I could show the ability of an officer of the Swiss army. At the end, I regretted I had outed myself as a Swiss Army officer. Of the whole group, I had the lowest score. The best shooters were the drivers. They could not hide their thorough army training!

One of the traditional instruments to confront North Koreans with other realities were the exposure trips, first to Switzerland and later to

Asian countries which were considered more relevant examples for North Korea. The participants were particularly impressed by Vietnam and considered that country as a model: opening up the economy while keeping a strict control politically and make sure that the elite remained in power. I had the chance

of accompanying a group in Switzerland. They followed the practice, they had learned from the Big or Dear Leader. They took notes whenever we stopped. Writing notes looked very much as part of their homework. Besides, they showed a genuine interest. When they saw someone working in the field, they wanted to interview the person. One of the participants was the Director General of Livestock. He was a quiet serious person, never speaking, always observing. All of a sudden, he burst out and asked me where all the Swiss cows were. He explained Swiss agriculture to me with facts and figures and the amount of cattle in the country. He presented details I didn't even know were available.

2.3.   Preparing for a Round-Table Meeting

The Framework conditions

The preparation of the documents for a Round Table Conference was the central part of the programme "Capacity Building for Enhanced Development Cooperation". These documents were waited for with the highest expectations. The donors expected robust papers enabling them to have the basis for switching from short term emergency assistance to long term development cooperation. The Koreans hoped for a first immediate step to rehabilitate the situation before 1994. At the same time, they made clear that their objective in terms of energy supply was the level of 1989.

All involved were aware that the success of the programme and the potential of a Round -Table Meeting depended on the outcome of the international negotiations at a higher level. The role and the status of the nuclear programme of North Korea were always present as a sword of

Damocles. Everyone was aware of the danger of a rupture at geopolitical level even when this eventuality was never spelled out.

Nevertheless, this situation had its concrete impact on the terms of reference for such a conference. The topics chosen by the government were energy and food security. As energy was evidently related with the nuclear issue, which, if included, would have blocked the whole process, the scope of the energy subprogram was reduced to "rural energy".

The second topic, food security, was at first sight an evident priority. The external players as well as the Government had relatively clear perceptions. Digging into this topic, we realised that though energy was politically very sensitive, food security proved to be even more controversial for the aid agencies.

Rural Energy

The text of the terms of reference for the preparation of the basic documentation for a possible round table was surprisingly non-problematic. But the organisation of the studies proved extremely difficult. UNDP considered rural energy as one of the priority areas in the overall program and had special funds from the Norwegian government. We ran into difficulties because the government refused all the candidates proposed by UNDP. The country director was desperate. He was not the only one who found this refusal to be proof of the lacking interest of the Korean Government. According to my contacts the Koreans did not want to have "development cooperation experts" with experience in third world countries.

The whole situation changed when we managed to convince the Swiss government to approve additional funds for hiring Swiss consultants. As I had already previously contacted potential experts, we were able to field a mission within weeks. Out of an UNDP mission it became now an UNDP-Swiss mission. Among the three experts was again our Vietnamese friend, with a Canadian passport, and two Swiss nationals. To the surprise of everyone, the mission had a good access to the authorities concerned and had good technical discussion partners. They received also data and statistics we never received of for agricultural production. I would not like to exaggerate the significance of the nationality of the mission members and the social dimension of the mission, the human relations. In practical terms, however, the fact that one of the team members was of Bolivian descent and was an excellent singer with confirmed experience in Karaoke singing, helped the mission to create an excellent environment.

The study produced by the experts together with their Korean colleagues proposed a three-year rehabilitation programme of the existing infrastructure. The focus was not the investment in new plants but modernising the national grid, energy saving and replacing some basic equipment. The proposal was very down to earth and concrete and I am convinced it was useful with and without development cooperation.

For me as a non-technical person, the data and statistics were just as interesting as the technical aspects. They showed the demographic development of North Korea based on the population census of 1993 (21.06 Mio) and assumed an annual growth of 1,5% which decreased after 1993 to roughly 1%.

More impressive were the figures for the energy sector. In 2000, the country produced only 27% of the energy it produced in 1989! Following the loss of the preferential treatment by former socialist countries the primary energy supply was reduced up to 1994 by 40%. It again declined by 40% since 1994 caused by the 1994/5 floods and the country's limited capacity to import oil and spare parts. This decline affected all sectors of the economy. Energy was lacking for irrigation and drainage and mechanical equipment. The fertiliser production declined between 1989 and 2000 from 458'000 metric tons to 28'000, a decline of 94 %.

The backbone of energy was coal. But the floods put some of the tunnels in the mines out of operation. The hydro power plants with one exception were built in the 30s and had never been modernised. I had the chance to accompany the consultants occasionally. Once we visited a construction site of a new power plant. According to the experts the plans were state of the art and corresponded to the technology of the 60s. I was amazed by the over-simple, labour-intensive construction methods.

Construction workers on a site for a power plant construction lifting bricks for the construction of the power house with the simplest possible means.

North Korea produced also its own turbines, which- according to our consultants- apparently had a 30% lower efficiency than in a modern environment. My impression was that not only the Korean authorities but also the technical staff were keen on getting support from abroad. Whenever I dropped into a meeting they were having lively discussions, brooding over construction plans and energy schemes. The need apparently helped to open the doors. Even when it was clear that the Round Table Meeting was politically dead the Korean government presented a detailed list with specific materials required to finish turbines under construction. UNDP could not respond positively to the request. The special material could also have been used for rocket construction.

Food security.

This was the topic where we from the project management were more directly involved. It had been a crucial issue from the foundation of the country and became the avenue through which some of the donor agencies came to North Korea.

First, we had to find a common ground with our Korean partners. For them, food security was an essential part of Juche, the national ideology. Self-sufficiency, as it was translated, was a central point for them and the ability not to depend on others for feeding its own population was an overreaching goal. The need to have the ability to supply food and being autonomous concerning nutrition was part of the founding myth of the country at the end of World War II. When Korea was split into North and South (on the 38° degree of latitude), the south was largely considered an agricultural country. According to studies published at the end of the 40s, North Korea was not viable as a state because of the non-existence of agricultural potential in the country. North and South were considered complementary, an ideal match.

One of the most important tasks of Kim Il Sung was to feed the population and not to be dependent on foreign sources of grain. The government made a tremendous effort to prove the experts wrong in spite of unfavourable agro-ecological conditions with long winters and very mountainous landscape. Where ever possible, the land was flattened and irrigation introduced. For the mechanization, the government started a campaign of retro-engineering: they decomposed imported equipment and reproduced it with their own resources. The modernization of agriculture was only possible through the high subsidies of the industrial sector.

The early 60s brought a new dimension to the food policy in the country. The arising conflict between the Soviet Union and China (military incidents on the Ussuri river) was not foreseen in the communist mind set and produced a crisis in the Korean perception of the world. Government and party introduced draconian measures. Juche was strengthened and consolidated into a national philosophy. The country opted for a third way of socialist development with a strong nationalist note. All the trainees abroad (especially those in the German Democratic Republic) were called back.

The core element of Juche was the introduction of a radical land reform, which changed the production pattern and should have generated sufficient food for its population. According to independent observers, DPRK reached some surprising results. The yields of rice and maize were comparable with the most advanced agriculture in East Asia. The agricultural development strategy was actually a classical Green Revolution package.

Seen retrospectively the production reported by the cooperatives reflected more the potential yields than the actual results in the field. In addition, the land reform had two serious setbacks. Firstly, it focused virtually exclusively on the production of carbon hydrates (maize and rice) and neglected the production of fats, protein and microelements. As a consequence, after more than 50 years, North Koreans are said to be 20 centimetres shorter than their brethren in the South. The second was that the system was not sustainable. The high consumption of energy and the overuse of chemicals actually questioned the economic and environmental viability of this system. High doses of fertilizer without organic material reduced soil fertility.

The North Korean agricultural system had already an embedded crisis when after 1991 the end of the COMECON reduced the traditional market of the industrial sector and cut the backbone for the support of the agriculture. The drought and floods in 1994/5 threw the whole country into a deep crisis.

The second challenge for the project team were the international donors represented by the agencies present in the country. The reason for their presence was hunger. Their entry into the country - with the exception of the KEDO partners - was provoked by the natural disasters. The damages of the floods somehow were evident but no official figures allowed a clear assessment to be made. The flood rehabilitation was soon mixed with the perception that the communist government was not able to feed its population. The lead agency was the World Food Programme, which had built up its largest programme worldwide. The status of food availability was regularly analysed by FAO/WFP with two special missions a year.

This perception of the food situation became an issue of controversy in our work. We gradually developed serious doubts about the quality of the FAO/WFP reports. As early as June 2002 I prepared an internal note voicing some doubts:

> "Concerning the general food situation: I think there is a general underreporting on food production in DPRK (and an over reporting of population figures as well as an underreporting of agricultural land). While agriculture remains critical and food supply depending heavily on climatic variations, I think the country manages to feed itself in a very good year in terms of grains.

This statement is based on the analysis of food production before 1945, the measures from 1945 to 1991 and since the crisis. Of course, the whole foreign community in Pyongyang will question this statement. In this regard, I had a short encounter with Roberto (the CTA of AREP). I think there are too many vested interests involved to allow or a clear analysis. The report on the food situation of FAO/WFP of 26 October 2001 includes contradicting information and I wonder why the quality of this report was not questioned.

The increased capacity for self-sufficiency is due largely to ecologically unsound practices probably since 1991: I have been deeply impressed by the high degree of sloping land cultivation. According to a report in the hands of Roberto the surface of slopes taken under cultivation has reached a surface between 550'000 and 600'000 ha between 1992 and 1999. During the last couple of years, this surface has considerably increased. Together with the intensification of the home gardening and all the sideline activities not considered by the FAO report of 2002, this constitutes an effective counterstrategy of the agricultural producers against the crisis. I have also some clear indicators that there is food available in the countryside. They do not fear an immediate shortage. However, there might be transportation problems.

The above-mentioned production as well as an increasing part of agriculture products goes to the farmer's market. Of course, there are no figures. According to the impression I gathered, the farms are very keen to produce for the market (they only talk in terms of market...). Selling this produce in the farmer's market is at least implicitly allowed by the 1998 constitution (art.24). However, the purchasing power of the city dwellers working in not operating industries has declined. They will suffer from a weakening PDS (Public Distribution System).

Emergency Aid and Rehabilitation might have a negative impact on economic recovery. Food distribution is giving new life to the highly centralized and inefficient PDS and is making competition to more effective distribution systems. But the importance of the system should not be underestimated for weaker segments of the society and in times of crisis.

Rehabilitation might be necessary in the short run. However, it functions under the premises that the old production system can be rehabilitated with appropriate investments. This is probably fundamentally wrong. The crisis of DPRK is not the result of a unique ecological event. It is part of changing overall frame conditions: The highly sophisticated irrigation schemes are the children of an age of very low energy prices. They are economically not any more viable. There are also indications that the irrigation potentials for paddy have been overstretched in the past. Since independence the government has tried everything to compensate the loss of paddy fields through the division of the peninsula. However, the agro climatic conditions were never favorable. Introducing new pumps and sophisticated tractors (as being done by the international NGOs with ECHO funding), will increase frustration and disappointment. Such programs should at least be accompanied with strong training programs. But in the long run DPRK needs a new policy of food security. In the midterm, the ecologically unsound cultivation practices are a means of survival. However, the donor community should make a substantial effort to introduce at least conservation oriented practices. The loss of forest will weaken substantially the capacity of the country to harness its water resources, which is one of the strategic assets of the country."

The underreporting of food production was enhanced by the new view of the FAO/WFP mission that agricultural production on land with a gradient above 15 degrees should not be considered as viable and discarded, a decision not hindering the farmers to continue to produce maize on steeper slopes. Our first impressions were confirmed in the discussion of an informal working group of all agronomists working in the different agencies. The CTA of AREP was part of the group and contributed actively to the analysis. As an employee of FAO, he was not ready to report these considerations. The findings were confirmed by the final report of the CTA of the EU fertilizer project. He was himself a professional maize grower. He had visited the fields regularly and made his own measurements. His data were substantially higher than indicated in the official reports. In addition, I had the information from the international reinsurance intermediary, which I could not use.

Apparently, what I thought was new, was widely known by others. Just nobody was interested. When I presented my findings to the Humanitarian Coordinator, the highest UN official in the country, he considered them as non-representative. He went to Peking. At a press conference, he made the statement everybody wanted to hear: 6 million inhabitants in DPRK are suffering from hunger.

The inconvenient Truth

As the person with the task to promote the switching from emergency to development cooperation I was more and more in the situation of a lonely missionary in an unfriendly environment. I remember two keys experiences:

Our colleagues from the Foreign Ministry invited us for dinner in a newly opened restaurant. We were a group of about 20 people, mainly Koreans but also UN representatives. We thoroughly enjoyed the different varieties of meat (a rare luxury!) and particularly the drinking. During the evening, the discussion around the table became continuously more animated among the nationals and somehow the expats remained silently in the background. From my neighbour, I understood that the topic was about emergency aid and development cooperation. It was apparently the continuation of a discussion they had had that afternoon in the ministry. My supervisor was very vocal but he was clearly in a minority which made him raise his voice even more. He was defending the need for abandoning short term emergency assistance and entering into a new type of relation with the foreign agencies. I was glad he defended well my agenda. The majority and surprisingly the younger officers clearly opted for a continuation of humanitarian assistance. Their main argument was that humanitarian assistance and food aid had no strings attached and left a lot of flexibility. Development cooperation came with conditionalities and the Koreans had not the slightest interest in letting the foreigners put their noses into Korean affairs. They saw no advantage in development cooperation and were convinced that the American government was not ready for change. So, with humanitarian assistance they got at least something. I was amazed that such a discussion took place during dinner. I had also the impression that this was not a vote for isolation. I knew too well the aspirations of the young officers and their admiration for western gadgets and behaviour. It was rather an expression of self-confidence "Don't worry we can do it".

The second ball fell into my camp. I invited the Ambassadors of the EU countries to a working dinner in our guest house. With my foreign colleagues, I had prepared a power point summing up our knowledge in terms of food situation in the country. My message was clear: the official figures by FAO/WFP presented an erroneous picture of the food security situation. In normal years, there was actually no justification for food aid to the country. It would be more effective to help by changing priorities and improving the quality of food (proteins, fats, micronutrients). My public listened very attentively. At the end of what I thought had been a brilliant presentation I missed the applause. After a moment of silence the ambassadors voiced their uneasiness. The conclusion of the evening was that we should not publish these figures. If we started questioning the usefulness of humanitarian assistance we would destroy the small bridge of communication which remained between the donor countries and North Korea. It was politically inconceivable for their governments to do anything but humanitarian assistance which per definition did not imply a policy discussion with the government but was targeting exclusively the needy population.

I had to accept that the Koreans as well as the foreign diplomats representing their respective countries wanted to continue humanitarian assistance in a situation where the objective situation would have required another type of relation. I also got a rebuke from my superiors: as an UNDP employee, it was not my task to question the specialized agency (FAO).

Consequently, the report we produced for the Round- Table Meeting was called "Rural Modernization for Food security and Broad-based Rural Development". It used the official figures presented by FAO/WFP, which, as everyone knew, were incorrect. As the macro-political situation deteriorated further, the Round-Table Meeting did not take place at all. I think the report on rural energy constituted a good guideline for the technical ministry. The report on rural modernization probably ended in a drawer of UNDP.

I ended my assignment with UNDP and went to Afghanistan. The United Nations continued   with a project for a certain time. I was succeeded by a real UN expert. From Kabul, I heard how American pressure was increasing. Wall Street Journal published an article accusing the North Korean government of misusing millions of dollars in foreign aid. As far as I knew all the UN projects, above all WFP but also AREP and IFAD as well as my project, were agency executed or implemented directly by UNDP. This means the funds and equipment were managed exclusively by the foreign agency. If there were misappropriation, they should have accused the UN personnel. In my project, there was just one window of opportunities for cheating: the project imported Toyota Jeeps. The Koreans completed the list with three sets of spare tyres, arguing they would have difficulties importing them later on. I was not aware of what happened with the spare tyres and never saw them. The UN operations officer who should have controlled this never made a report. So the modest programme of UN in North Korea got suspended with not very convincing arguments.

During the following years North Korea fared well without World Food Program assistance.

3. Vote for Engagement

3.1. Common Wisdom Questioned

How resilient is the System?

For the Korean pundits, food security was not just an issue of agriculture: hunger in North Korea was largely used as an indicator for the stability of the system. It was commonly accepted that the regime was about to collapse. At least it was considered as a proof that the regime was not in a position to feed its population.

I have tried to show that after 1999, North Korea produced enough food. The deficiency was rather the one-sided promotion of carbon hydrates and the neglecting of proteins, fats and minerals, which created a structural deficit in the nutrition of the population. Hunger, for a long time seen as the weak point of North Korea, was on the one hand the picture the outside world wanted to see and the Korean Government wanted to show.

A second series of indicators are the defectors. The total number is estimated by American sources between 25 and 30'000. They usually get a high profile in the West and are occasionally even invited to the White House. Vice President Pence, while attending the opening ceremony of the Olympic Games, was proud to meet defectors even with the risk that a meeting with the North Korean emissary would be cancelled. We in the West see in the life stories of individuals a sign of frustration and revolt against an authoritarian and directive system.

Is such a system with a rigid top down centralized government with a strong personality cult viable? Seen with Western eyes we tend to come to negative conclusions. The question is whether our perception, woven with the western value system, is actually doing justice to local reality. Even Cha, in his well-researched publications, mentions that North Korean defectors surprisingly do not often mention the repressive system or the lack of liberty but economic suffering as reasons to flee the country.

Historically speaking the people in North Korea have known feudalism, then foreign domination, and since World War II, an authoritarian system. This is not the environment   which creates liberalism and freedom- loving citizens.

Certainly, governance in North Korea is authoritarian and strictly controlled. It is what we like to associate with the classical communist system. But we tend to ignore that the history and geographical situation as well as the geopolitical situation of North East Asia have influenced the system as well. The mechanisms of governance are not only influenced by myths and "Marxist-Leninist" legacy. Neo-Confucianism, with which the leadership is playing with virtuosity, the anti-colonial heritage and history have shaped today's power structure. There is not only the supreme leader endowed with a personality cult, but also the army and the workers' organisation, which have their own political weight in decision making.

All these forces are also supported by a strong nationalist feeling which tends to be corroborated by the geopolitical environment and a high concern of the elite not to lose its privileges.

In North Korea, there are not only the hard-line communists, but there have always been   representatives of the old nationalist bourgeoisie who helped to fight the colonial power. The University of foreign languages is probably still a breeding place for a new generation of leaders linked to these origins. Future historians might be interested in analysing the family stories of the alumni of this university.

Reading about past times, it is surprising how much the present regime has copied/ pasted from the historical legacy. Personality cult is not just a new phenomenon. If it looks rather out of this world in the western perception and value system, it is much more familiar to the Korean soul. A very often quoted example for the expression of the personality cult in North Korea is when the leader is shown with either the top brass of the army, the cabinet or the party leaders. Everybody is standing in a circle around the leader listening very attentively and taking notes. When I was accompanying a delegation of civil servants to Switzerland, we visited the underground powerhouse of a hydro-electric complex. Our guests were listening very attentively to the explanation of the engineer. I am sure they did not understand more than I did. However, they were all taking notes assiduously. This attitude is very familiar to those who are studying the social system in the old China. First, you have to pay respects to the master, secondly you have to acquire knowledge. This is the basis for your promotion and thirdly, the traditional system means that if you have acquired knowledge about something from a book or notes, you are expected to know how to use it. But application in the traditional system was not the practical use but to show your knowledge in the exam which decided on your social promotion. In other words, neo-Confucianism is very present in today's Korea and is having its impact on everyday life.

Juche, self-reliance, with its three dimensions, is considered the philosophical base of North Korea. It is meant to give the North Koreans a national ideological framework. For us Westerners, it is hardly understandable. We see inconsistencies and the whole Juche discourse looks artificial. This might be symbolised by the Juche tower overlooking Taedong River. Besides, the fine view the westerners are most interested by the high speed of the elevator taking the visitors to the top. In the contact with Koreans I had the impression it was more than just propaganda. It has certainly been a masterpiece of invention by the great Leader to devise a national ideology when the two socialist mentor countries, China and the Soviet Union, started to fight each other on the

Ussuri river. To see Juche as an invention just for the outside world, as some authors suggest, is just a foreign misinterpretation.

I remember when someone on visit to South Korea brought back a leaflet prepared for the introduction of foreigners who wanted to do business in the South. The Vademecum, we thought, could be applied to the letter to persons wanting to work in North Korea.

In conclusion: The North Korean system has a basis which is much stronger than the communist ideological and organisational heritage. It is also rooted in Korean history and culture. This has to be taken into account for anyone wanting to connect with the country. It is quite unfortunate that American academia, so famous for its independent analysis, but also functionaries of the administration, focus their attention on what happens after the fall of the present system (see the opening hypothesis of research initiated in 2016 in the US-Korea Institute of John Hopkins University). Actually, for decades, high ranking Americans have continued to announce the end of the North Korean system. Being citizen of a superpower apparently does not enable one to penetrate the realities of a small and not always very easy country.

Is Reform possible?

In 2001/2, we were always looking for the big decisions and the breakthrough for the reforms we thought so urgent. They would have helped to eliminate central bottle necks of cooperation and would have given a new working basis for the international community. But alas, the big change did not take place and the persons working in North Korea had to fight with increasing frustration.

Looking more closely at how the country overcame the food crisis, we had to accept that there was a lot of unexpected flexibility and ingenuity. In addition to the measures mentioned in this paper, North Korea had leased land in Siberia so that Koreans could there produce food grain to feed its population. The government had organised free trade zones with China and South Korea and had sent labourers to work in the Siberian forests.

More importantly, the agricultural system based on the green revolution package in the early sixties had gradually and silently been replaced by a better adapted and more decentralised system exploiting environmental differences and differentiating the seeds according to their agro-ecological potentials. At first seeds were imported from Switzerland, but these were gradually replaced by imports from other countries, e.g. China had developed maize varieties with even shorter vegetation periods, and the Netherlands had potato seeds with higher starch content. The Swiss replaced their agroforestry consultants by people from the China office of ICRAF.

The chronic deficit of micronutrients and vitamins was compensated by Soybean plantations on the borders of rice fields, the promotion of small livestock and vegetables was a regular feature of educational TV programs.

Our reading of the situation was that the official "niet" to proposals was often accompanied   by serious study. All of a sudden, certain changes were applied without ever communicating a decision or admitting that change was required. When the Swiss helped to organise the first international potato conference, the international experts were astonished to meet highly knowledgeable and experienced Korean scientists with a scientific background of potatoes.

There were also some fundamental changes taking place: the government distribution system gradually lost its importance and served only needy people. The amount of agricultural production being marketed outside the official system increased. I mentioned above that factory workers and retired persons were planting maize on sloping fields. Apparently, the overreaching objective was to produce sufficient food. Even if the government had not officially taken a decision it was clear that they could do it only with the approval of the authorities.

Some authors analyse the situation of North Korea in the perspective of the end of the Cold War and the end of the socialist systems in Eastern Europe. Professor Kim of the Kyung University Changwon makes the difference between the Chinese and the Russian models: China conducted a "regime reform", maintaining the political system and introducing market economy. Russia made a "Regime change", changing the economic as well as the political system. He sees in North Korea a "low-level regime reform".

Our view was that the overriding mantra of the North Korean was to be in-charge and never to admit that they accepted an improvement suggested by foreign devils! Yet they are very alert. No authority would ever question the past agriculture policy of the Great Leader, even though the daily practice is being changed rather swiftly.

The economic policies and daily behaviour in North Korea are much more flexible than the external observer is aware of. Yet it remains far away from a market economy with a free democratic political system, as some observers dream of. The role models of the region and the proper history will push the country in its own direction.

Vocally Extreme - Pragmatic in Daily Life.

Listening to the few emissions in English on the radio, looking at TV or reading government statements, the harsh tone and the overstressing of national pride as well as the almost obsessive need to convince the listener rather by strong wording than by arguments, was always disturbing. It seemed to be a ritual of the official communication policy.

This sometimes frightening way of communication looked as if offending potentially important negotiation partners was part of the game. Apparently, the authorities did not shy away from the consequences. The tone is such that you would never expect any discussion was possible (actually President Trump seems to be a quick learner: his way of communication follows similar lines).

This official line of conduct seems to be in contradiction to the way problems are finally solved. At operational level the Koreans are much more pragmatic. They seem to be shooting high in order to prepare for arrangements at a practical level.

It is an attitude one can also observe in the endless (and, frankly speaking, boring) speeches the Great Leader used to make on his tour to the cooperatives. He did not insist on the impossible and was rather educational. If you want to know the real agricultural yield of rice and maize, you should not go to the exhibition of socialist heroism in Pyongyang, you should rather read Kim Il Sung. In his speeches, he is addressing the concrete difficulties, making suggestions for the improvement and criticising the enormous waste in terms of postharvest losses.

My impression is that the often abusive and offensive use of terms and the sometimes insulting treatment of certain foreign leaders will not hinder the Koreans in having contact and negotiate with those whom they are shaming officially.

The Perception of the Neighbours

South Korea is probably still considered as a puppet state of the US. They created South Korea and are responsible for the separation of the Korean nation into two countries. They favoured a militarisation of the South with General Syngman Rhee as a first president and the military regime until the late 80s. There are still strong pan-Korean tendencies on both sides of the 38th parallel and the North tries ruthlessly to exploit all signs of nationalism (and anti -Americanism) in the South. The recent campaign of charm and the invitation of the South Korean president are well calculated gestures. The trans-Korean reflex is being mobilized but the real customers are the US.

China saved the DPRK in the Korean war and sacrificed thousands of lives. China is in certain respects the big brother who is annoyed by the bad behaviour of the younger brother. But North Korea does not like the position of the younger brother. There is a love-hate relationship. Historically speaking China and Korea have had strong cultural and economic links. The Koreans used to pay tribute to the Chinese emperor in the same way as the Tibetans did. Thus, the relation can be characterized by respect but also fear. I observed in personal contacts a certain uneasiness of Koreans to talk about China and their relationship with the big neighbour. They are impressed by the recent economic success of China. They have achieved what North Korea dreams about: economic growth and success without questioning the power structure. Chinese support of the war of Kim Il Sung was not out of sympathy for North Korea. But they did not want the Americans ante portas. The North Koreans know how to play this keyboard and have so far been successful in using it. The big neighbour is not amused at all.

Relations with the **Russians** are much older. Kim Il Sung was supported by the KOMINTERN in Manchuria. Under Stalin during World War II,

KOMINTERN had already taken a more nationalist turn and Korea was definitely not on their radar during the war. When the Russians landed in Wonsan after the sudden armistice with the Japanese, they didn't even have Korean speaking persons among their troops and had to mobilize emigrated Koreans from Central Asia. Kim Il Sung became an essential asset to deal with the Koreans. He was the Rhee of the South in the North with the exception that he could boast of an anticolonial involvement in Manchuria. Rhee in the South had just his American background as an asset and was thoroughly hated in the North as well as in the South. Kim knew well that he was only on the periphery of Soviet Interests. The way he managed to lure the hesitant Stalin into the Korean War was a masterpiece of conviction (based partly on wrong assumptions). Stalin had enough worries with the western most socialist satellite, East Germany. That's why he consented to engage only the Air Force. The Koreans know that today's Russia is quite far away in terms of political priorities. Engaging the Russians helps them to play a more important role globally and to be an active part of the negotiations.

Japan is endowed with all the negative characteristics of the former colonial power. They are associated with the suppression of Korean culture, the abuse of Korean women during the war and for discriminating the Korean colony in Japan. Even today, Koreans in Japan are considered as second- class citizens. For the Koreans, it is clear the Japanese have to make a big and costly effort to make the Koreans forget all their misdeeds. (Objectively speaking the Japanese made substantial contributions to modernize Korea and to build up an industry in the north). The prevailing mood in Japan is not much inclined to concede this to the Koreans.

I have had the impression that **Vietnam** was the Shangri-la for the North Koreans. The lady ambassador from Vietnam in Pyongyang was treated like a princess, and when the Swiss reoriented the exposure trips to Vietnam, the participants were quite enthusiastic. Vietnam enjoyed a very positive image:

- They were economically very successful under the control of the prevailing elite and sticking to the existing power structure.
- Vietnam was a relatively small country bordering China and had the courage to follow its own path. They were even militarily successful against the Chinese.
- Vietnam has managed to participate successfully in the global market.

I suspected that also the positive bias in favour of the Swiss was due to the will of independence and traditionally following its own path: they were culturally conservative and economically very successful. The North Korean saw a certain similarity with the Swiss and surprisingly the national-conservative politicians in Switzerland had a hidden sympathy for the authoritarian system in North-East Asia.

The **United States** are genuinely considered the culprits for anything going wrong with North Korea: they were responsible for splitting the Korean nation and were the leading party in the Korean War. They were the ones who put pressure on the European countries and the UN system on the way to boycotting the country. While urban youth admires American fashion and western modernity, they would rather stick to the present system than opening up and suffering American dominance.

For the North Koreans, the Americans are not reliable. They quote as an example the Frameworks Agreement negotiated by the Clinton administration but never approved by Congress. This might be an analysis shared by other members of the six party talks. The Chinese in particular never hid their position of insisting that the Americans were as much part of the problem and the solution for a peaceful development in Korea. The Korean view is that the US are no model for good governance and democracy. I remember when a French NGO published a report on human rights violation in North Korea and mentioned 125'000 political prisoners, the number was not questioned by the North Koreans. According to them normal delinquency and politically "incorrect behaviour" is not always clearly separated, and both, according to North Korean ideology, need re-education.

Considering the average number of the population in prison in North Korea, in 2004 the percentage in the US was even higher. Irrespective the harsh and repressive attitude of the Korean authorities, there are no news of having as many North Koreans killed by police in the streets as in the United States.

In spite of this critical assessment, the North Koreans are convinced, a peaceful and sustainable development on the Korean Peninsula requires a settlement with the United States. Being able to discuss with the Americans at the same eye height has been a strategic objective of the leadership at least since the end of the Cold War.

3.2. North Korea's stumbling towards Recognition

Preliminaries

The following lines can be considered as pure speculation. I cannot quote reliable sources and what I am writing certainly does not belong to the mainstream thinking and to what politicians like to hear. Actually, I never had the intention to write such a paper and the little sources and papers I had, landed in the waste paper basket a long time ago. The following lines are therefore based on memory and personal interpretation.

For the parties concerned, and particularly the United States, there are probably three basic options: continuing to isolate the country by sharpening the international boycott, engaging in negotiations bilaterally or as part of the six party talks, and the third would be initiating military action.

Even though the leaders of North Korea and the United States boast of having the nuclear button close to their night lamp and are competing about the size of this button, the war option should be dropped. The assumption is that both main parties consider the risks of military solutions as too big. It would eventually generate at least a regional war with all the neighbours engaged. Before discussing solutions, I think I should put in writing what I consider some basic driving forces which characterize the political behaviour of the country.

The Nuclear Temptation

Kim Il Sung wanted to have nuclear technology. The justification given was the need for energy, an argument today's observers might agree with. However North Korea always had a wealth of coal mines (though partly coal of low quality) and a potential of hydropower which remained unexploited. In addition, the prevailing attitude of society allows a waste of energy which could be reduced at little cost. Actually, energy was considered a public good. No incentives existed using energy in a rational way. The argument of lacking energy has become valid only since the end of the Cold War. The game with nuclear technology is older.

Even though the army and the militarization of the country was a kind of birthday present put into the cradle of North Korea at its creation, I advance the thesis that the nuclear bomb was not the initial motivation. I see the reasons for going nuclear much more in Kim's value system and his perception of the world. His bible was the historic materialism, basically a materialistic and positivistic view of the world typically prevailing in the 19th century. The basic axiom is that thanks to science man can dominate nature. Nature has to be formed to serve mankind. It is also what we perceive today as the basic attitude among young Koreans that modern technology will solve all the problems.

In Kims view, Korea has the human resources to make the country a scientifically leading country. This is all the more necessary as the country is not endowed with rich agro-ecological resources. Science will help to overcome this deficit. Nuclear technology was top notch after World War II and Kim wanted to be on top and have a nuclear plant. This ambition to be scientifically and technologically up-to-date characterizes the industrial development but also the agricultural policy of North Korea. Kim did not see farmers, but workers engaged in production according to scientific criteria. The agricultural reform 1960-64 follows the slogan chemicalization- mechanization-energy. He flattened the land wherever he could and introduced highly expensive irrigation systems (where water had to be lifted by electricity-driven pumps in up to twelve stages) based on energy at zero cost. Of course, the advocates of Green Revolution found in Kim a very loyal and consistent practitioner.

The decline of the system did not start with the natural disasters. They were the culmination. It started with the economic slowdown of the COMECON countries, the reduced subsidies from the Soviet Union and increasing energy prices. Fertilizer factories had to close down, the soils spoilt by overdose of fertilizer and agrochemicals no longer yielded as expected. [26]

My impression: the purpose for North Korea in having nuclear technology to start with was the satisfaction of owning a top technology and showing that the country was a technologically leading nation

The End of the Cold War

During the Brezhnev period the economic slowdown of the COMECON countries had already been felt. This resulted in reduced support for the socialist frontier country in the east and a limited outlet for Korean industry. While North Korea had supported development projects in Africa including rice cultivation in Tanzania and Uganda, and during a few years was even a rice exporter, at the end of the 80s the surplus converted into a deficit. According to the international statistics of IRRI, North Korea started to import rice from Thailand.

With the end of Cold War, North Korea lost not only the subsidies from the socialist countries but also the market for its industrial products. For the leadership, the consequence was clear: the country had to be integrated into the world economy. Speeches of the Great Leader clearly indicated the new direction. There was even a party decision, approving a resolution for the participation in the international exchange of goods and services.

The free world was of course not waiting for a new player in North East Asia with its special agenda. All the socialist countries - with the exception of Albania and North Korea - had abandoned their heritage of the

---

[26] As a typical anecdote: the cabbage, the main raw material for the basis of Korean cuisine, kimchee, in Pyongyang suffered dramatically because of an insect. This fly had become resistant to the agrochemical applied. The Swiss, with the help of CAB (the Commonwealth Bureau of Agriculture), introduced natural enemies combatting the insects.

Second World War. For North Korea, it was clear: integration yes, but conservation of its own political system is a must! Actually, the Koreans wanted what China practiced: access to the world market but keeping its own political system.

The nuclear power with an old and hazardous technology and the danger that North Korea was building a bomb became the asset North Korea used in the negotiations. The compromise was the Framework Agreement of 1994. North Korea got what it needed most after the end of the Cold War: food aid, fertilizer and energy! Korea was to abandon its nuclear plant and discontinue the nuclear research. Part of the compromise was also the building by KEDO (Korean Peninsula Energy Development Organisation) of a hydrogen energy plant in North Korea.

With the end of Cold War, the nuclear capacity had become an important negotiation asset with the neighbouring countries and particularly the US.

North Korea Part of the Axis of Evil

2002 promised to be the annus mirabilis. In July reform measures were decided. Though in the immediate term we did not welcome them with much enthusiasm. We were hoping for more and had doubts how serious certain measures were really meant and whether they would be implemented at all. But we felt there were strong indications that the leadership considered ending nuclear development. Our strongest indication was our Vietnamese friend. We had included him as an economist in our energy analysis and planning team and he was back as a consultant. He was repeatedly visited by three young good looking and well-dressed men for some confidential talk. Twice he was invited to a kind of brain-storming with some inner circle of the leadership: the topic was how some 500 highly specialized researchers in nuclear technology could be reoriented.

In September, the Japanese Prime Minister visited Pyongyang. The expectations ran very high. He presented excuses for the abuse of Korean women during World War II. Following this statement, the North Koreans expected high compensation payments following the example applied in South Korea. The North Korean leadership admitted for the first time the abduction of Japanese nationals. What was thought of as part of a détente from the North Korean side, created in Japan an outcry of indignation. How could the Prime Minister envisage compensation to a regime which had been responsible for such a crime. Though this visit is today considered as an important step, at the time deep disappointment was felt.

These developments were overshadowed by the State of the Union Speech by President Bush in January. North Korea was declared to be part of the Axis of Evil. The chances for a settlement and the end of UN sanctions quickly evaporated.

The Koreans must have seen themselves confirmed in their policy of the Shogun: "Army First". The new administration with its declaration, and the invasion of IRAQ showed the Koreans the high risk and danger of an invasion.

While the CIA director was predicting the fall of the regime within three years, the people of North Korea were possibly never so united behind their leadership. Sacrificing personal comfort for the defence of the country must have become a moral obligation. The build-up of the military capacity was accelerated with a new dimension.

Missiles and Nuclear Capacity a threat to the US?

According to reliable information from various sources, the Korean population is better off than ever in the last almost thirty years. Probably the most impressive source of information is the book by Felix Abt.

During the last 15 years, in spite of all sanctions imposed, North Korea has further developed its military strength. In addition to the nuclear bomb they have managed very quickly to beef up their ballistic technology with missiles apparently having the capacity to reach US soil and carry a nuclear bomb.

The latest development has been accompanied by a verbal confrontation between the two leaders in Korea and the United States, and to the surprise of the general public, they seem to have found a common style in throwing insults at each other.

Under the surface of the new confrontational attitude on both sides, we might neglect

developments within the country. The supposed low level "regime reforms" have been accelerated, and the terms "communist" and "Marxist-Leninist" have been deleted in policy papers. Abt mentions the disappearance of the portraits of Marx and Lenin from the building façade of the Foreign Trade Ministry. In North Korea, such symbolic acts always have a deeper meaning. There are clear indications that Shogun (Army first) policy has lost its priority against economic development and the wellbeing of people. Strong, conservative military leaders have been replaced and the party is becoming more important.

This internal change is accompanied by an offensive of charm at the Olympic Games. I interpret this as a way for North Korea to improve relations with the South. However, the important elephant in the room remains the United States.

Dealing with the elephant, in the perception of the North Koreans only strength will be understood. Those who expect that North Korea will reduce the importance of this important trump card are underestimating North Korean determination.

3.3. Policy Alternatives

The Blunder of American Diplomacy in North Korea.

For thirty years the American government, Korean pundits and even Academia have been singing the gospel of the immediate fall of the North Korean government and its system. A Japanese author observes that the number of studies on North Korea is enormous, most of them are authored by Americans, but virtually none of the authors speaks Korean and most have only a very superficial knowledge of the country[27]. The main concern of researchers is not to understand North Korea, its way of functioning and inner logic, but to find out what might happen after the fall of North Korea[28].

Victor Cha in his book on North Korea[29] can certainly not be accused of lacking knowledge about the "Hermit Kingdom". The book is very well researched, which is documented by 40 pages of bibliographical and source notes. It abounds with detailed knowledge about the country. As a professor of a renowned University, staff member of the National Security Council and advisor to President Bush, he was very well positioned to give an insight into the functioning of the North Korean System. Behind this wealth of detail and scientific glossary, we detect the simple and convenient truth: North Korea is deemed to fall and the system has no future. This statement appears repeatedly in the text. In vain the reader looks for a clear justification. This raises questions about

---

[27] Atsuhito Isozaki, Understanding the North Korean Regime, Wilson Center 2016.

[28] The US- Korea Institute of John Hopkins University launched in 2016 a research program with this central question.

[29] Victor Cha, The Impossible State, North Korea Past and Future, London 2013

the scientific basis of the analysis. The frequent value statements confirm the doubt whether this is really an honestly researched book or a political justification. I wonder whether it is the difficulty of eminent thinkers of a world power to understand how a small state ticks, which has been constituting not much more than a nuisance for American interests. In his book, there is hardly a mention of the constraints of American interior politics, which have been creating a serious hurdle for finding a solution to the present tensions. It is therefore no surprise that Cha does not see a concrete solution, but to "wait and see". The United States should demonstrate patience and watch the system falling apart. In many papers and above all newspaper articles we observe little effort to understand and accept a certain reality. There is a systematic effort to emphasize the negative news, to make a fool of the leadership in place and a lack of respect for a completely different reality.

In spite of all negative predictions, North Korea seems to fare better than ever since the end of the Cold War. The sanctions imposed by the UN following American initiatives have not brought the results its authors expected. A strategy of wait and see is highly risky and hasn't brought us closer to a peaceful situation on the Korean Peninsula.

The strategic thinking of containment of the American governments of the 60s and 70s might teach a lesson. Assuming that the future dominance will come from China (actually they have laid the basis in terms of raw material, technology, political leadership and ideology), the counterstrategy should not be to weaken the neighbours but rather to help them develop their own identity. This will probably be the most effective strategy to counter the hegemony of one single power. A good example is certainly Vietnam. Another could be North Korea. Unfortunately, the isolation of this country has steadily increased the Chinese influence and reduced their economic and political potential for self-sustained development.

Sanctions are not Effective

The question is, why are the sanction measures not more effective. In an article published by the Korean Journal of Defence (Analysis Vol.10 No.3, 2014 quoted by Vantage Point Sept). 2014) the author states: "Even though the UN sanctions aimed at discouraging North Korea from developing nuclear and missile programs and taking action that threatens regional peace, it has not effectively served its purpose". At the beginning of 2018 they should be more effective than ever. Yet there is no indication that North Korea will change its position due to the latest measures. It is evident that since the foundation of the country in1948, and particularly after the end of COMECON, DPRK had to show a high level of imagination, flexibility and ruthless habit to exploit the slightest niche which was opened. This created again and again tensions and conflicts. North Korean diplomats used their position to make money also against the ethics of western values. However, they had clear targets to reach: the embassies had to finance themselves by the means available. They are running restaurants, engaging in international business and seizing every possibility to make money. The North Koreans have become masters of improvisation.

Supporting all these internal and external efforts by the Koreans, there are a number of external, even global factors which help the county to survive in spite all the international sanctions.

In general, the UN member countries are not compliant. First there are the series of "rogue" states (Syria, Iran, Myanmar etc.) Then, the ASEAN states do not like the instrument of sanctions and apply it only very loosely. More importantly, China as well as Russia weigh their interest in regional stability higher than the importance of the international sanctions decided by the Security Council. They clearly see the US as partly responsible for the unruly behaviour of the North Koreans.

Globalization is another important factor. It is creating loopholes for any international boycott. This is apparently a disadvantage of the absence of a global governance, which could constitute an internationally compelling framework. We observe that multilateralism is rather retreating. The international concert of nations has not a single director, there are even different orchestras not playing the same tone. It does not make it easier that the states are not the only player in a globalized world. Transnational companies have grown in size and power. No state in the capitalist world is willing to impose restrictions on these companies. Possible directives are based on voluntary actions and self-discipline. Both are moral principles which belong to the mantra of the capitalist world. The behaviour of the states are concerned with the creation of the best possible legal and tax environment to lure as many international players into its territory. Controls by the states in this context are not popular. This situation creates openings and flexibilities weakening any effort of international boycott.

Internationalization of trade, communication and production have become the main features of globalization. As explained above, the governments of the western world are not inclined to limit the freedom of the global companies. The growing of China as an economic and political power, the recovery of Russia, as well as some autocratically led newly industrialized countries are developing a new behaviour pattern. The relation between the state and internationally active companies is not transparent. We suppose that there are very close financial, personal and operational linkages. Contrary to the free world, these companies operate clearly within the realm of strategic objectives set by the state, the dominant party or a charismatic leader. These companies have been expanding globally. They secure the access to raw materials and land for the future of their country of origin. In industrialized countries, they acquire companies or at least majorities in the assets of technologically attractive and for the economic expansion of their country essential knowhow. This development has its impact on the Korean Peninsula: the mother country of these companies can easily approve international sanctions. Whether their companies behave accordingly remains an open question.

Negotiations

How to deal with North Koreans? Thinking about this, I think basic lessons learnt and guided by common sense and sound human behaviour are applicable also here.

All the same, there might be some specificities to be considered:

1. In 2003 the SDC representative in Pyongyang came back from a trip to Seoul. He brought back a leaflet prepared by some Korean business association prepared for new comers showing how to behave for dealing successfully with – Koreans. We were of the opinion the paper could be used for the introduction of anyone going to North Korea. In other words, there are common cultural features which might be as strong as the communist heritage. We are in Korea. My neighbour back home has travelled widely in Eastern Asia. He found the Koreans very difficult business partners compared with the Chinese: arrogant, basing their knowledge less on practical experience than book knowledge, hard minded, selfish and continuously looking for their advantage in each step.

2. Whenever we had critical issues to be discussed with the authorities requiring green light from a higher level, there were basically two approaches. When the frustration was particularly high on the international side, a list of the points to be discussed was established. When the meeting took place, the responsible person did not show up. He sent one of his collaborators. The meeting took a very formal and rather stiff turn.

At the end minutes were drawn which the Korean had actually prepared beforehand. The conclusion of my UN superiors was that the government was uncooperative and unwilling.

The second approach was to meet for dinner or in another informal context and to discuss the issues informally. The important thing was to establish first an atmosphere of informality and confidence. This gives the persons involved the chance to have internal consultations, till a position has been defined. All the same the minutes were prepared beforehand but the person in charge showed up personally. I think this has to do with the concern to protect oneself in the hierarchy and not losing face.

So, in North Korea we are in Asia. Personal relations help to open doors and to prepare the territory for more flexibility.

3. In all major issues, we quite naively expected the "breakthrough", which of course never happened. We had the impression that the Koreans examined proposals very carefully and sometimes clearly applied what had been proposed but without ever accepting a proposal. I think there are two features to be considered: the Korean partner does not like to accept what outsiders propose. This creates the impression of undue dependency. But there is yet another critical point. I never had the impression that a great decision was made overnight. Even minor things had to be carefully cleared with different power centres and the interest of the stakeholders carefully balanced. Our impression was that the inner circle of the leadership was the most open. The midlevel staff had internalized the socialist rigidity and believed in the ill will of the foreign devils. They were highly sceptical and resistant to change. I never had the impression that the supreme Leader could take frank and clear decisions. There was a need for consulting different hierarchies. In such a situation, you can never expect spectacular results. If they are, the probability that they are reverted next day is high. Successful

negotiations need patience, a lot of energy in relation and confidence building and time to make sure all the internal power cells have their advantage.

4.   North Koreans, like other people with a strong nationalist and isolationist past, are very proud and present themselves as self-confident. Maybe my view is somehow biased in this regard: I was employed by the United Nations Development Programme. For the perception of the Koreans, this programme is meant for developing countries in Africa and elsewhere. The North Koreans saw themselves as being citizens of an industrialized country. The Country Director of UNDP, a Bangladeshi, was at every possible occasion given to understand that they did not   need advice from anyone coming from a country like Bangladesh.

North Korea wants to avoid by any means having to discuss any precondition for negotiations. But this has also a psychological and subjective aspect: they want to be considered as equal partners.

Confrontation versus Engagement

Trying to sum up development in Northeast Asia and interpret the situation in an emotionally loaded environment, where propaganda and short-term politics tend to hide long-term visions and evolutions, is very tempting. Reality is never that clear

and in the influence of many contradicting factors, and it is just not possible to draw a simple red line. Nevertheless, concluding a subjective and personal interpretation of what happened in North Korea since the end of Cold War, I shall try to make an oversimplified summary:

- The sanctions against North Korea have gradually become stiffer and stiffer. North Korea, and particularly its population, are suffering. Scarcity is the buzz word. However, we do not have the impression that the North Korean determination has weakened.
- The prediction by so called "trustworthy" sources, mainly in the United States, announcing the imminent fall of the North Korean system has become with the years more precise and focussed on the present. However, at the same time, the well-being of the population seems to improve. Again and again, indications of a weakening grip of power by the ruling elite seem to be premature.
- With the sanctions imposed, the dependency of North Korea on China has steadily increased. Strategically speaking this is not a desired outcome. A lesson learnt from the Vietnam War could be that strengthening the autonomy of small countries surrounded by big neighbours would be more promising than continuously weakening them.
- The military strength of North Korea in terms of threatening capacity in turn has been strengthened. In 1994 the issue was mainly nuclear technology and the danger of the bomb. In 2004 the bomb was a reality. The question was, how its importance can be mitigated. The issue was, what are the North Koreans going to do with it. In 2018 the bomb has become somehow a fact that has to be accepted. But in the meantime, this bomb can be carried by North Korean missiles as far as the United States.
- With the end of the Cold War, the Free World celebrated the victory of capitalism. The author of the book announcing the end of history was the celebrated herald. In 2018, we realise that the world continued to change. The nexus between free market economy and democracy, the mantra of the Free World at the end of the Cold War is shattered. In East Asia, China has become the dominant player, economically and politically. It has become the main investor in emerging countries

like Malaysia, Indonesia and the Philippines and the US have increasingly lost their pre-eminence and have now retired to the role of "America First". The change of the United States could not be more dramatic. It was symbolically demonstrated when President Obama could not attend the ASEA conference in Indonesia because of a government shutdown back home. The majority of Republicans in Congress implicitly considered home politics higher than external interests of the country. In the meantime, XI Jingping was touring the capitals, promising new investments. The administration Trump has pulled out of the Free Trade negotiations with the Pacific states and declared that America will not any more defend human rights and Western style democratic systems. This could create positive framework conditions for negotiations: if President Trump really meant what he said it will be easier to bring the North Koreans to the negotiation table. The downside of it all is that the United States want a settlement because they feel threatened by the North Korean missiles. No great world power likes to negotiate in a situation of weakness. This makes today's situation frightening, despite the charm offensive during the Olympic Games.

3.4. Why President Trump might succeed

On 9 March 2018, President Trump was invited by the leader of North Korea to visit his country. Practically they will meet somewhere. I think the chances for a positive outcome are real:

North Korea has reached its strategic goal: it is recognised as a partner at eye level with the United States.

More importantly, the situation in the United States under President Trump is unique:

- The President has a republican majority in Congress. The chance that an agreement with North Korea would be accepted is better than ever since 1991.
- The President means business. No moral strings attached. This makes negotiations much easier.
- The President is well known for his unorthodox positions and has no problem in ignoring traditional antecedents.
- The North Korean threat has become a kind of political hype in the United States. Defusing the danger would be an enormous gain of internal prestige.
- President Trump can already position himself for the next election: Russia with Putin re-elected for the coming years and Xi Jing Ping elected for ever will give Trump arguments that the United States need a similar leader to defend American interests in future.
- Finally, the last person engaging for peace on the Korean Peninsula was Kim Dae-jung, the president of South Korea. He was rewarded with the Nobel Prize for Peace. Such an international recognition would boost the ego of the American president as global peace bringer.

However, President Trump has to win a difficult steeple chase. The American public and the internal politics in the country but also within the White House could prove to be higher hurdles than the stubbornness of North Koreans.

Selected Bibliography:

Andrei Lankov, The real North Korea. Life and Politics in the Failed Stalinist Utopia. Oxford University press 2012.

Andrei Lankov From Stalin to Kim Il Sung. The Formation of North Korea 1945-1960. Rutgers University Press 2002.

Atsuhito Isozaki, Understanding the North Korean Regime. Wilson Center 2017

Charles K. Amstrong, The North Korean Revolution 1945-1950. Cornell University Press. 2003

Felix Abt, A capitalist in North Korea. 2013 (2016)

Gavan Mc Cormack, Target North Korea. Pushing North Korea to the Brink of Nuclear

Catastrophe. Nation Books. 2004.

Hermann Lautensach, Korea, Land- Volk- Schicksal. Koehler Verlag Stuttgart. 1950

Jonathan Brent, Inside the Stalin Archives. Discovering the New Russia. Atlas&Co.2008

Kim Jong Il, On the Juche Philosophy. Pyongyang 2002

Kim Il Sung Works, 30 Volumes.

Kim Jong Il, For the Victory of the Socialist Cause, Pyongyang 1999.

Kim Il Sung, A travers le siècle. No.8. Pyonyang 1998

Kim Il Sung, De la gestion de l'économie socialiste. Pyonyang 1992.

Martin Fritz, Schauplatz Nordkorea, Das Pulverfass im Fernen Osten. Herder Spektrum. 2004

Mike Chinoy, Meltdown, The Inside Story of the North Korean Crisis. Saint Martin's Griffin New York 2008.

Michael Breen, Kim Jong Il: North Korea's Dear Leader. John Wiley &sons.2004.

Nada Takashi, Korea in Kim Jong Il's Era. Pyongyang 2000.

Pierre Rigoulot, Nordkorea, Steinzeit Kommunismus und Atomwaffen-Anatomie einer Krise. Kipenheuer & Witsch. 2003

Rüdiger Frank, Nord Korea, Innenansichten eines totalen Staates. Deutsche Verlags-Anstalt. München 2014.

Willliam Stüeck, Rethinking the Korean War. A New Diplomatic and Strategic History. Princeton University Press 2002.

Vantage Point 2002- 2016

Victor Cha, Krys Lee, The Impossible State. North Korea Past and Future.

Young-Key Kim-Renaud, König Sejong der Grosse, Der Glanz Koreas im 15. Jahrhundert. Edition Peperkorn. 1997